The Voyage & The Return
THE PATH TO SELF DISCOVERY

NICOLETTE HALLADAY   CATRYN BECKER

ASHLEY SHELDON-GATES   TANIA ORMONDE

MAGGIE MOORE   JENNIFER FAI ARMITAGE

VALERIA MARITZA   CAROLINE BENGTSON

TARA CAMPBELL   KIM TREMBLAY

ALLISON KRAWIEC-THAYER   APRIL AZZOLINO

JAMIE WAREHAM   MOIRA CAMINO   STEPHANIE OLIVO

RUTH ANN KRISA   REBEKAH MEREDITH

Inspired Hearts
Publishing

Copyright © 2022 by Nicolette Halladay and Inspired Hearts Publishing

All rights reserved. Apart from any fair dealing for the purposes of research or private study, or criticism or review as permitted under the Copyright, Designs, and Patents Act 1988, this publication may only be reproduced, stored, or transmitted, in any form or means, with the prior permission in writing of the copyright owner, or in the case of the reprographic reproduction in accordance with the terms of licenses issued by Copyright Licensing Agency. Enquires concerning reproduction outside those terms should be sent to the publisher.

Table of Contents

Introduction	v
1. What does it mean to live a good life? *Nicolette Halladay*	1
About the Author	11
2. My Higher Self Saved My Life *Allison Krawiec-Thayer*	13
About the Author	17
3. DREAM, SURRENDER, THEN CREATE *A Story of Listening to Your Heart, Letting Go, and Having Faith* Catryn Becker	19
About the Author	35
4. Change of Heart - A Love Story *Kim Tremblay*	37
About the Author	45
5. 555 - A Story Of Faith, Resilience, And Change *Jamie Wareham*	47
About the Author	55
6. Total Life Reboot *Caroline Bengtson*	57
About the Author	65
7. Trusting My Inner Knowing *April Azzolino*	67
About the Author	71
8. Connecting to the Voice of our Soul *Tara Campbell*	73
About the Author	81
9. Forging Rebirth *Maggie Moore*	83
About the Author	93
10. THE DARKEST NIGHTS *Moira Camino*	95
About the Author	99

11. A Rose Blooms When You're Ready *Jennifer Fai Armitage*	101
About the Author	111
12. "They said, No" *Stephanie Olivo*	113
About the Author	119
13. You Are Not Crazy, You're Connected *Valeria Maritza*	121
About the Author	129
14. WANDERING WOMAN AT HEART *Ruth Ann Krisa*	131
About the Author	135
15. Through Darkness Comes Light *Ashley Sheldon-Gates*	137
About the Author	145
16. Dreaming over Blank Pages *Rebekah Meredith*	147
About the Author	151
17. The Inside Job *Tania Ormonde*	153
About the Author	163
18. Message From the Publisher	165

Introduction

In a world that often feels uncertain, it can be easy to lose sight of what truly matters. We may find ourselves chasing after things that don't make us happy or holding onto relationships that are no longer good for us. But what if we could learn to follow our heart's true desires? What if we could find the courage to let go of what's holding us back and sail towards the life we've always wanted?

The Voyage & The Return is a book about doing just that. It's a collection of stories about finding true love, following your dreams, and discovering your authentic self. Each story is an inspiration for anyone who has ever felt lost or stuck in their life. It's a reminder that no matter where you are on your journey, it's always possible to find your way back home.

In this book, 17 women share their inspiring stories about what it looks like to live an authentic life. From confronting their fears and doubts, to making peace with their past, to learning to love themselves unconditionally, they offer a powerful reminder that we all have the potential to lead lives of meaning and purpose by living authentically. It requires courage, but it is a worthwhile endeavor. These women show us that the rewards are more than worth the effort.

It is my great hope that this book will provide you with hours of enjoyment. The stories within are some of my personal favorites, and I have been privileged to play a small role in bringing them to life. I want to thank you for taking the time to read this book. I know that there are many demands on your time, and I am honored that you have chosen to spend some of it reading this book. I hope that you will find the stories within entertaining, insightful, and thought-provoking. Thank you again for your time, and I hope that you enjoy the book.

With love,

Nicolette Halladay

CHAPTER 1
What does it mean to live a good life?
NICOLETTE HALLADAY

The Portal

The idea for this book came to me on a cold December day, snuggled up in front of the fire with folded strips of paper laid out in front of me. Each paper had a different title written on it. I had just published my first book, Mystics Revealed, and was trying to decide on my next book title. There were several book title ideas swirling around in my head, but I was carefully considering what type of experience I wanted to encounter, almost hesitantly mulling over the options. You see, I have discovered that producing these books opens up a portal of sorts. An invitation to lean in and fully believe that you have the authority, the wisdom, the knowledge, the expertise to share these types of stories around this specific topic. I'm not sure if it's the unconscious mind bringing up old beliefs about our worth or some sort of external energetic force making sure we remember to solidify our beliefs, but there is definitely something to this. And not just me; I have spoken to multiple publishing colleagues who have reported a similar phenomenon. It goes something like this.

I want to write a book called "Mystics Revealed," and I'll share unconventional success stories from extraordinary leaders.

"Oh, you want to write a book about mystics being revealed, do you?" We'll definitely be testing your belief and ability to trust, surrender, and manifest your reality. " Next thing you know, different challenges are popping up to test you.

A decisive decision is always a good decision.

I had settled on 3 to 4 different themes but was finding it hard to make the final decision. I remembered this decision-making tool that a mentor had suggested to me several months ago when it came to deciding between multiple options. You write each possibility down on a piece of paper, fold it up, and put the paper in a container. You pick one of the folded choices and that is your answer. It can be that easy! As long as you can get behind it 100%, you know you have picked the right one. A decisive decision is always a good decision.

Imagine my surprise when the paper I picked up had the words "A Voyage and the Return," which wasn't one of the titles I had written down. What the heck? I flipped over the paper and… nothing. I hurried over to my desk and realized the notecards I had used to write down the titles had notes from a previous training on the other side. The Voyage and the Return is a framework for storytelling. Think of *The Wizard of Oz* or *Alice in Wonderland*. The main character ventures into the unknown, and at first, the world of the unknown is fascinating and exciting. They face challenges but inevitably overcome them. I had somehow cut the end off one of my notecards with these words written on it and included it in the container I was pulling from.

I wasn't sure what to make of it. Obviously, there is a message here. I thought, "I should tell The Voyage & The Return type of stories." "Stories of women who have been on these types of journeys." OK, I sat with it for a while until finally, it smacked right into my being. You asked for the title and this is what came through. This title is being handed to you on a silver platter. If you can't take this nudge, which is more like a blatant push, do you even believe in synchronicities or universal messages? And for the skeptics out there (you seriously can't make this stuff up.)

And so it was decided-*The Voyage & The Return* would be the title, with the subtitle *The Path to Self Discovery* coming through shortly after. And it made sense. I had been on my own voyage over the last year. My 24-year partnership with my husband suddenly came to an end, starting a publishing company, driving across the country to heal my heart, and slowly but surely coming home to myself.

"These are the kinds of stories I want to share," I thought. Stories of incredible women who have been on voyages and how that experience brought them back home to themselves.

But this chapter is not about the previous 12 months or that voyage that shook me to my core, flipping the world as I knew it on its head. That story has already been shared in several previous books, across social media platforms, and poured out into my personal journals.

Nope, I want this story to be a wake-up call, a battle cry to all of you who are living a life on autopilot. A predictable life that looks exactly the same as the day before, minus the weekends, which look just like the last weekend you experienced. Those of you who wake up unhappy most days, who are going through the motions of life but not really living it. A reminder to all of us that we don't have to be thrust into or embark on some extraordinary voyage in order to live a great life. We can choose any moment to take that journey back home to ourselves. We get to decide.

I hope you remember the power you have to choose yourself each and every day. You have the power. The power to wake up each morning and prioritize your happiness. To ask yourself one of the simplest and yet most profound questions you can ever ask yourself, "What does it mean to live a good life?" And "How can I experience that today?"

Since the early days of my separation from my husband, I have had the good fortune to be surrounded by the most incredible and dynamic women. Passionate women who were running profitable online businesses and making it a priority to live their best lives. Many of these women have also experienced some sort of grief or sorrow in their lives. So they weren't saying "life is always unicorns, rainbows, and sprinkles, get over it." They were insistent on choosing themselves every single day.

It was refreshing to always be reminded of the power we have to make today a great day. Or reminded that there is plenty of time to take today and heal. Feeling good, doing things that we enjoy, and filling up our cup is the same magic pill we need to take in order to create our best life or grieve for a life we once loved. I believe that prioritizing my joy significantly shortened the time I needed to heal my heart after my marriage ended, and it has given me a roadmap to follow when it comes to intentionally choosing a life to be proud to wake up to each day. I want to share some of those concepts with you.

Turning off the news.

Within days of my husband leaving, I turned off the news. It was almost a gut reaction to deal with the grief I was experiencing. I could no longer handle the barrage of negativity streaming into my reality. I insulated myself into a cocoon and took back control of the things that could fill my consciousness. I needed to focus on the things I could control, and the things being discussed on the news were so far out of my control that they were putting me into a constant state of flight or fight. For those of you who worry that you might miss some important event—you won't. I usually hear about major world events from someone, and that keeps me informed enough. Shortly after the news was turned off, I stopped watching TV altogether. Significantly limiting the media's influence in my life was a massive confidence boost. I stopped comparing myself to other people and started to appreciate myself again. The real version of me. The one who had been buried under all those layers of expectations for so many years. It was incredibly freeing.

Commit to meditating every single day. And some days I meditate twice.

I had picked up Joe Dispenza's book "Breaking The Habit of Being Yourself" and was doing the work to let go of the smaller parts of myself to make room for the bigger parts of myself to materialize. People often ask, "How do you have time to meditate so much?" and I usually say something like, "I can't afford not to." Those hours I spend in mediation are sometimes the only moments of peace I experience all day. I can always tap into joy and happiness during my meditation, so I know that I can experience more of that when I'm not meditating as well.

Countless hours spent in nature with absolutely no agenda.

I sometimes spend hours sitting under a tree, watching the leaves blow in the wind and down to the ground, watching the birds fly in and explore what could be found. My admiration for trees really blossomed. I never paid much attention to trees before, but all of a sudden I found myself enamored with them and started giving them the reverence they deserved. I often go for long walks, stopping at each flower that crosses my path to admire its beauty and smell its lovely scent. I have sat by lakes and rivers and begged these massive bodies of water to tell me how to heal my heart. For some reason, I always thought that the water would know. I love to move in and out of the water, pick a rock to lie on, stack stones by the creek, and just let the water wash over me. If all those hours observing nature have taught me one thing, it is this: *nature doesn't have to try to be anything other than what it is. It is just perfect, and so are we.*

I bring nature inside.

I am always looking for ways to bring nature inside, and because I don't have a natural green thumb, I have to get creative. Me and houseplants have a checkered past. I'm working on it.

There are a few easy ways I have found to bring nature inside.

- I seek out and sit in the light.
- Every morning, I open the curtains wide so the sunlight can flow in.
- I light candles and just watch the spark of the flame dance.
- I sit in silence by the fireplace and allow myself to feel enamored by the strength and light of the fire.

Flowers help me feel alive.

I regularly purchase fresh flowers. I found that many local grocery stores have clearance flowers available for a fraction of the cost of retail. I bought four bouquets for under $12.00 and have made it a point to treat myself to fresh flowers on a regular basis. When the flowers start to wilt, I'll add them to my bath water for an indulgent bathing experience.

Put yourself out there—life is waiting to be lived.

My life has drastically changed from being tethered to my children and never having a moment to myself to going weeks without them and being completely alone. And because I own my own business and work from home, I found myself alone a lot of the time, and it started to suffocate me. "Oh, you're back." I would scoff at myself as I woke up in the morning.

I scoured the internet for local events and found some meetup groups to join. I added all the events that even somewhat interested me to my calendar, so I always have something to do. Even if I just go to a local show by myself and enjoy something delicious to eat, at least I am surrounded by other people who are also enjoying themselves. I found one meetup group that I really clicked with called *Toast & Trails*—they hike sometimes or get together for dinner. The majority of them are new to town or recently returned, so there's a lot of diversity in people and perspectives. It's been a great way to meet new people and check out some new places. Having the events in my calendar has also come in handy for the weeks I spend with my girls because we always have fun things to do together. These are new and different things that we would have missed if it wasn't for this proactive approach.

Nurture your relationships.

I've become much closer to my friends because I am always making sure to stay in touch and have learned to ask for help or advice when I need it. I share what I am experiencing more freely. I let go of a lot of guards I had up, thinking that I had to make things look like they were perfect. Things are never perfect, so why even pretend? It's made for much richer friendships with much more depth and understanding.

I have learned to reach out to existing friends much more often and get things scheduled. Like every Wednesday, I go hiking with one of my friends. It's been a welcome mid-week reprieve for both of us. Reaching out and being the one who is inviting people, planning get-togethers, etc. not only enriches your life but adds value to other people's lives as well. You never really know what someone else is going through. Your invitation might be an answer to their prayers.

Become a YES Girl!

Did you know that the thoughts you have today are **95%** the same as the thoughts you had yesterday? Partly because we are living the same day over and over and over again. Besides the annual vacation, which many people spend worrying about the things that make up their day-to-day lives (that 95%).

I have become a YES girl. If someone invites me to share time, if there is a chance to connect with other people, experience an adventure, or even just get out of the house and it works with my schedule, I have made a commitment to say "yes" first unless there's a good reason not to. If I can make it work, I will. Which is the polar opposite of how I lived for a long time, having an immediate negative reaction and needing to be persuaded to say yes. Now it's almost always an automatic **yes** for me. I'm putting out to the Universe that I am open to new experiences and invitations as well as actively seeking them out. I'm hoping to break 95% of the same thoughts and create some new ones.

It is natural for you to feel discomfort between who you are now and what you are becoming.

This idea *that we are not good enough* can keep us stuck in our tracks with zero progress for years, and sometimes a lifetime. For me, it has shown up as multiple starts and stops to different business endeavors and projects and a whole lot of "deer in headlights" episodes. I would get an idea, get excited about it, dump a lot of energy and sometimes money into it, and then, all of a sudden, I would freeze. I couldn't move forward and didn't know how to get over my fear. What I realized is that when I was experiencing that fear, that discomfort, that disbelief that this was happening to me again. I was moving through some kind of growth. And it is so normal for us to feel discomfort between who we are now and who we are becoming. I didn't realize that then, but I understand it now. What I also realized is that when I was feeling that fear and letting it stop me from moving forward, I was making it more about me than about anything else. This often shows up as the perfectionist, the procrastinator, the "oh my God, what will people think if I suck or what does this mean for me if I succeed?" I hate to break it to you, but you aren't really that important. People are way more interested in their own lives and what they are going to get out of something than they are in how we look while delivering it. The trick for me has been to literally get over my own bullshit and out of my own way. Focusing on the why "Why does this matter?" To me, to my clients, and to the world, this has been a much more valuable and empowering position. It opens us up to potential and possibilities. Powerful choices we may never get to if we stay stuck on ourselves with thoughts of, "how this is going to make us look and feel?"

You are so supported

You might call it God, the Universe, Ala, The All-Mighty, Mother Earth, or something else, but connecting to and trusting this divine energy force makes living life so much more meaningful. The depths of what you will receive are so much greater. And whether or not you believe in angels, spirit guides, your ancestors, or your higher self, I hope you know that you are SO SUPPORTED and always guided by friends, family, colleagues, your children, and pets. There is ALWAYS someone there to support you. Trust and know that, always.

You are your biggest advocate.

Spending so much time, energy, and attention devoted to myself and my own fulfillment was not a super easy transition for me. After a lifetime of putting other people before myself, it felt strange to start each day asking—"how can I be happy today?" But what started as a lifeline to move through my grief has evolved into deep levels of fulfillment, purpose, and passion for me, but also permission for those around me to advocate for their own happiness, their own passion, and their own purpose. I have demonstrated what it looks like when you prioritize yourself and am inviting you to give it a try. No one is going to do this for you. It takes you to be intentional and sometimes courageous each and every day. I believe that if each person asked themselves these simple yet profound questions every day, then the world would be a better place for it.

What does it mean to live a good life?

About the Author

NICOLETTE HALLADAY

Nicolette Halladay is a 5 times international best selling author and 1 time best selling publisher of the book Mystics Revealed: Unconventional Success Stories from Extraordinary Leaders. The founder of Inspired Hearts Publishing. She gives business owners a platform to leverage their personal story, experience and expertise, grow their audience, and establish themselves as an expert in their industry.

She started her entrepreneurial journey by launching a virtual assistant agency where she learned the fundamentals of online business and found her love for publishing through niching down and exclusively supporting other female-owned publishers.

Nicolette has a deep passion for her work because of the financial and creative freedoms offered in entrepreneurship. Her love for this work inspires her clients to explore and express complete self-expression of their heart and soul.

Website: www.inspiredheartspublishing.com

Facebook: www.facebook.com/nikki.richardsonhalladay

Instagram: www.instagram.com/nicolettehalladay111

linkedin: www.linkedin.com/in/nikki-halladay

CHAPTER 2
My Higher Self Saved My Life
ALLISON KRAWIEC-THAYER

I saw my hand shaking as I dialed and prayed he'd see the call.

It was late September 2018, and I was huddled over the couch in my San Francisco high-rise apartment surrounded by dumpster furniture and Craigslist Ikea. I felt the world closing in and my thoughts getting darker. I'd been side-hustling as a coach for a year and a half and had never even had a *potential* client.

I'd been here before. I remembered feeling lost and aimless during my corporate years, but coaching and entrepreneurship were supposed to be the answer — wasn't it destined from the start?

The start was June 2016, when my father (to whom I was incredibly close) passed away from cancer at 56 years old. In the week following his death, I found coaching for the first time. Days later, I reached out to a certification program. As the admissions woman told me the price, I felt my heart sink. "I already have student loans. I have to wait."

Then came that true moment of destiny, when not even a day later, my mom called with the news that my father had a life insurance policy, and I would be receiving enough to pay in full for the program AND pay down my student loans.

From the moment I desired to go all-in on coaching, I was supported.

Yet on that dreary autumn afternoon, as I pressed my face against the floor-to-ceiling window staring at the San Francisco street below me, it felt like I'd blown my inheritance for nothing. I can't be a coach for people. I can't even figure myself out. Coaching was supposed to be my path, purpose, and direction, but I just can't cut it.

I was desperate for validation that I wasn't making a huge mistake, that I wasn't being selfish and wasting my life, and that I wasn't sabotaging my marriage by burning through Mitchell's savings. I wanted so badly to believe in my own future and to know that I was doing the right thing.

In the weeks leading up to this point, I noticed my anxiety building steadily. I found myself popping Lorazepam earlier and earlier in the day. I disappeared into episodes of Parks and Rec for hours. Now I realize how unsafe building a business truly felt to me at that point, and I'm not surprised that it came to a head that day.

I felt my brain searching desperately for my future, my path, a stepping stone. *"Life is a series of eventual panic attacks. You will never escape this."* My thoughts turned on me. I started to imagine the peacefulness of a future I didn't have to live in. The peacefulness of falling into traffic or someone with a gun breaking in and ending my existence. It just seemed so easy.

And at that moment, something that I both can and cannot explain happened.

I saw my hand, which I couldn't actually feel, was shaking, and I noticed myself calling my spouse. I was praying he'd see the call, but also feeling a weightless safety like the blue sky above storm clouds. As Mitchell answered, I heard myself calmly, yet firmly, tell him that he needs to come home immediately.

My hands then navigated to a browser and began texting a suicide hotline (because whatever had taken over me was honoring the severity of where we were). As the hotline person kept me company while waiting for Mitchell to get home, I started to research the process of checking into in-patient mental health care. I learned what was in-network with our insurance and the ER we would need to check-in through. I then calmly began packing my coziest clothes (even calmly noting to remove the drawstrings and select laceless shoes). I scanned my bookshelf, packed my toiletries, and grabbed my stuffed dog, Stella.

Moments later, Mitchell came flying in with his bike on his shoulder and embraced me in a hug, asking what's wrong.

"I need help and am going to in-patient for a while."

In those darkest lows, something Divine rose up and took over to calmly and precisely navigate us to safety. I was reminded of who I am and what I came here for.

Feeling back into the energy of that day, I can note the Divine in the room so clearly. I see my higher self and angels standing not 8 feet away from where I was crumpled over the couch, sullen and surrendering.

My higher self, my future self, the me who is destined to impact the world, she was there and literally guided me through. And she hasn't left my side in the years since I have continued doing this work.

As I stood pressed against the glass that day, I was calling out for a guide — someone or something to tell me that I wasn't messing up. And, as always, the best guide came from within. She showed up for my future. She let me rest while she navigated us to safety.

And safety came as four days of in-patient care with a balance of mood stabilizers, daily mindfulness, tai chi practices, card games, and movie nights with beautiful souls. It came as four weeks of out-patient care where I learned Dialectical Behavior Therapy tools to manage my emotions. It continues to come now in the form of trauma-healing EMDR therapy with my spiritual therapist, Kate, and my own meditation practice and daily connection to Source.

And now, I love my life. I wake up every day grounded in adoration for who I am and what I do. I have risen from the darkness, and through the healing of my hurts, I invite others to do the same.

A prayer to your Higher Self:

"May I feel your presence when you draw near, and may I bask in the abundance and ease of your greatness. May I embody your love in this world and be reminded of my own greatness as we become one."

About the Author
ALLISON KRAWIEC-THAYER

Allison Krawiec-Thayer is a certified energy leadership coach and specializes in spiritual business mindset. Allison reminds empathic entrepreneurs, heart-centered healers, and cosmic creatives who they are and what they came here for.

She has been featured in *Go Solo, Lovely Impact, and Authority Magazine*. Like many empaths, she grew up learning to people-please and serve others. This led to the teacher's pet, college degree, corporate job, and promotion trajectory. However, by mid-2016, she was fed up and longed for the freedom of entrepreneurship. And despite a seeming kismet flow of events, as her chapter shares, entrepreneurship didn't exactly go as planned at first.

Since this dark night of the soul, Allison has found her purpose and she daily gives thanks for the charmed life she now enjoys. She calls the front range of the rocky mountains home with her spouse and their 2 big-eared rescue dogs.

Connect with Allison via her website: www.poppylead.com.

CHAPTER 3
Dream, Surrender, then Create

A STORY OF LISTENING TO YOUR HEART, LETTING GO, AND HAVING FAITH

CATRYN BECKER

Scan here to listen along as the author as she reads her chapter.

With laughter filling my ears, I turn my head to glance down the sleek table inlaid with copper to gaze in wonderment at the smiling strangers. The unfamiliar lilt of the words and cadence of the speech reminds me that I am in a foreign land, yet somehow I feel more at home and at peace and just a sense of "rightness" than I have in such a long time. Maybe it is the decadence of the four-course meal or maybe it is the warmth of the whisky, but I know that I am exactly where I am meant to be at this moment.

"How did I get here?" I ask myself. How did I get to Scotland, of all places? To my knowledge, I do not have a drop of Scottish ancestry coursing through my body and, throughout all my worldly travels, Scotland has never been on my radar. I knew nothing about the place other than tired, well-worn tropes about kilts, bagpipes, and haggis. Yet ever since that fateful moment in April 2021, Scotland has been calling to me. Loudly and incessantly. Showing up in the strangest places. And now, 10 months later, I am dining with the Master Distiller of one of the top luxury whisky distilleries in Scotland and receiving job offers from his leadership team.

The dining room at the Glenmorangie House

Let's start at the beginning.

I am not going back all the way to the *beginning* beginning, but let's just set the stage. I am a good girl. I follow the rules. Well, for the most part, but more on that later. I do the things and take the expected next steps.

I graduated from high school, went to college, got a good job and an apartment after college. I pursued a career that would provide stability and security. A job that is needed everywhere. I am an engineer. Eventually, I met a nice boy. We dated, got engaged, got married, and had babies. We bought a house with a yard. We got a dog. I was living the quintessential American Dream.

I was... content. Ish.

I had this gurgling feeling that I kept pushing way deep down that I was playing small. I could just feel that I was meant for so much more than what I was doing, but somehow that felt arrogant to even think it, never mind say it out loud. Because remember, I am a good girl. I take others into account. I don't want to hurt any feelings or step on any toes.

Yet, I had this burning desire to help others lead better lives. I wanted to help in a more tangible way other than the engineering work I was doing. But I couldn't give up being an engineer and the financial contribution it provided my family. That would be irresponsible. After all, I had worked so hard for all those degrees and promotions. I couldn't just give it up. In 2015, my mind was expanded when I was introduced to the power of essential oils through a company called doTERRA. Here was a way, I thought, that I could supplement and maybe one day replace my engineering salary, all while getting to help people! Score! And it was fun. I loved teaching classes and showing people who were skeptical (as I had been) what these amazing plants could do.

I did this for several years and achieved small milestones here and there that kept me engaged, striving, and more or less satisfied. But I wasn't growing at nearly the rate that I desired, and I couldn't figure out why. As an engineer, I really like to figure things out, and it is frustrating when I can't see the solution. I felt as if maybe I was delusional by thinking I was meant for more since this business, which I thought was my 'way out', wasn't working the way I thought it should . How could I control this situation?

At some point along the way, I was given the advice that networking is a great tool for increasing awareness to get more sales. Engineers don't network. This was a completely foreign concept to me. Going to conferences made sense to me, but not this structured networking situation, but since I was entering new territory, I thought why not! I was invited to join an online BNI group. I didn't even know what the acronym stood for and had no clue what was expected of me during the meeting, but I could feel a big heck yes in my soul, so I went. I mostly felt out of place but there was one person in the group who grabbed my attention. She was a life coach and used a method created by Coral Grant called the Subconscious Release Technique (SRT). It was life changing. I started seeing the coach and was having the best months in doTERRA that I had ever had. My mind was alive with creativity and inspiration about new ways to serve people to make the changes needed to achieve their goals. But what I noticed was that even though I was improving my processes and making it easier than ever for people to attain their physical and emotional goals, there were still mental obstacles preventing them from taking action. It was like they felt they weren't worthy to live that kind of life. It was at this moment that I knew I needed to incorporate SRT into my process. It was time to become a coach.

My Meeting with a Warrior Goddess - April 2021 - The Poconos

To feel the music, listen to the Last of the Mohicans soundtrack.

In early 2021, I learned of a retreat called Love Warrior. This retreat was being hosted by Brianne Hovey, an amazing leader in doTERRA. I had attended one of her live workshops a few years prior, and I had friends attend many other workshops and retreats, but I just hadn't felt called to attend them myself. But something about this retreat was different. I knew I was transitioning from doTERRA being my sole focus to just being a piece of it as I grew as a life coach and partner with SRT Global. So I was surprised when a doTERRA-centric retreat caught my attention. I just *knew* I needed to be there, even though my logical mind couldn't make sense of the why. I could come up with a list as long as my arm of reasons why NOT to go and very few reasons why I should. At the time, I had this fuzzy idea of how I could introduce Brianne to SRT and maybe it could help my new business take off. In the months and weeks leading up to the retreat, I kept trying to force a SRT session with Brianne, but it just never worked out. At the very least, maybe I could do some sessions with the other attendees at the retreat and gain clients that way. Yes, yet another example of me trying to force and control the situation.

Channeling my inner warrior at the Love Warrior Retreat

I asked my great friend and doTERRA buddy, Lacy, if she would like to go with me. To my complete surprise, Lacy was kind of on the fence about it. This shocked me since Lacy had attended a different Brianne retreat called Elevate the year before and RAVED about it. I really wanted Lacy there. I think it was out of fear of the unknown that it would be more comfortable to have a friend. It can be scary to do something you have never done, where you know no one.

Well, the idea I had in my mind of how the retreat would go was nothing like what actually happened! Brianne had the retreat designed in such a way that we first peeled back the layers to uncover our inner Warrior Goddess, since most women have an underdeveloped warrior archetype. She led us through a meditation where we were standing in a power stance with our eyes closed with the "Main Theme" from the Last of the Mohicans playing in the background. As the music swells, her words are swirling in my brain. My heart is pounding in time with the music. My breathing gets faster. An image starts to emerge from the darkness of my mind. It is a woman. A very powerful woman. She is confident. She is a badass. Her hair is braided and messy. Bri is still walking among us in the room, but I can barely hear her. It feels like it is just me and this warrior – the rest of the room is fading away.

"What is your name?
What should I call you?"

I ask. I see her lips turn into a wry smile, and she answers me. My brain cannot make sense of what I hear. It sounds like Sarah, but I have a deep knowingness that it is not Sarah. She says it again, and I still can't make it out. Brianne slowly guides us back into the room and out of our reverie. I am excited yet confused and eager to learn more. I need to figure this out, but we aren't supposed to use our cell phones during the retreat, and now we are on to the next event. Later that day, I could not stop thinking about my warrior. I decided to dig out my phone to do some light research. Due to my Irish ancestry, I thought maybe the vision was connected to Ireland so I started searching there. To my dismay, I didn't really find much. There was only one name I could find that even started with a "S", and it didn't look anything like Sarah, that much I was sure of. I put my phone away and continued with the retreat. But it still nagged at me. I had more time the next day to dive back into my research. I had the inspiration to go back to find the one S name – Scáthach – and see if I could find a pronunciation of it. And there it was. The phonetic pronunciation is SKA-hah. That was the name I heard! I dove in to learn more! Her name means Shadowy One, and she allegedly lived on the Isle of Skye in Scotland. She was the goddess of healing, magic, martial arts, and prophecy. It was at this moment that I knew I needed to go to the Isle of Skye.

Taking the Leap

Not only did the Love Warrior Retreat plant the seed to visit Scotland, it also sparked a flame, a new vision, between Lacy and I. My friendship with Lacy began in my mid-20's. We had mutual friends, and to be honest, it was a pretty shallow relationship that mostly revolved around being at the same bar at the same time. The friendship deepened and evolved, however, as I discovered essential oils. Through social media, I had learned that Lacy was on her own wellness journey, and I thought doTERRA might be a good fit for her. Turns out, it was a great fit. We began to interact more in this area and made several pilgrimages to Salt Lake City for the annual convention. As I began to explore SRT, Lacy was learning more about another modality called Emotion Code and a coaching method focused on understanding the Clifton Strengths. Our doTERRA relationship grew from one of mentor and mentee to holding weekly mastermind sessions. We each were inspired by the other and loved bouncing ideas back and forth. After our time together at Love Warrior, our communication soared from weekly to nearly daily. We began in earnest to use each other's services and saw quantum leaps in our progress. We had something major on our hands. Individually, we were great, but together we were magic. We wanted a company name that represented that what we do is an ever evolving process and the end result will be unique for each person. And so, Journey 2 Cloud 9 was born. Through the combination of our modalities, training, and experience, Journey 2 Cloud 9 guides those in the midst of a midlife crisis to discover, understand, and appreciate who they truly were created to be.

Journey 2 — Cloud 9

Leading up to Scotland

I fully committed to my new life of coaching and was able to create enough income to make our trip to Scotland, specifically the Isle of Skye, a reality. My favorite number has been 22 since I was in high school, so it just seemed perfect to take this trip in the year 2022. Eric and I discussed timing and decided that February would be the best time for his schedule. February. In Scotland. If you know anything about Scotland in February, you will know that this is not a great time to visit. Like literally the worst month to visit. I was slightly disappointed but just so happy to start planning the trip. One morning, through a discussion with my kids, I realized that I could be in Scotland on February 22, 2022. 02-22-2022! How perfect!?! So it was set. I have the Dream. What I didn't realize is that I would experience moment after moment of learning to surrender and give it to God.

Surrender Opportunity #1 –

Eric was happy to go and do whatever I wanted in Scotland. He just had one request – to visit the Glenmorangie Distillery. Which is on the complete other side of the country. Granted, it isn't a huge country but it definitely put a kink in my plans. I *really* wanted to control the situation. In my research, I discovered that there is a bed and breakfast associated with the distillery, fittingly called The Glenmorangie House. The rooms looked absolutely luxurious in the photos, but what really sealed the deal was the ability to attend a tasting of four single cask whiskies, exclusive to the House. I knew we had to do it – it would make Eric so happy. Happy Birthday, babe! And anniversary. And Father's day. (It was a splurge for sure!) Based on the flights we had selected, the best day to stay at the House would be Monday. This made all my plans work out. But it was sold out on Monday. Ugh! The ONLY day available that week was Wednesday. Right smack in the middle of our trip. This will just not do. I fought it for weeks, and I tried to find other ways for the trip to fit MY design. I finally sat back, with a great sigh, and said "fine." Wednesday it is. I will make everything else work around this. Time to give it to God.

Surrender Opportunity #2 –

Covid had never stopped being a concern, but I was holding faith that it would work out, somehow, someway. And then Omicron happened. Everything was shutting down again, and we were only two months away from leaving. Would we still be able to go? I was obsessively checking the websites for the UK and Germany (where we would make our connection). It was so frustrating as the rules for testing were in a constant state of flux. Each country had a different timeline as when testing was done and used different words to describe what tests were necessary. As we got closer and closer, the rules started to settle down, and it looked like it would all work out. We only needed a negative PCR test taken within 48 hrs of our flight in order to enter Germany. We could do that! I scheduled our appointments exactly 47 hours and 35 minutes before our flight as I wanted the maximum allotted time to get our results back. It had been 31 hours and still nothing. I was starting to panic. I reached out to Coral, the founder of SRT Global, for a private coaching session. (Because we all need coaches in our lives!) My distress over the situation was palatable – you could hear it in my voice and read it all over my face. Coral asked me the most perfect question.

"Have you done your part?" she asked.
I was a bit confused, and I began to rattle off all the things I had done. She asked again, "Have you done your part?"
"Yes," I answered, "I have done everything I can."
"Great. Then **give it to God***. Whether it works out or not, it is above your pay grade now."*

I sat back in my chair, blinking furiously. She was absolutely right. I had done everything I could, and the rest was out of my hands. I took a big sigh of relief. It felt so good to let go of all that angst and put my energy and faith into trusting God and His infinite wisdom. Coral and I continued our session, and of course, I felt so much better, as I do after every SRT session. I picked up my phone as I left my office and felt it vibrate. It was an email notification from CVS that my results came back as negative. I had the biggest smile on my face and so much peace and joy in my heart. Scotland was a go!

The Juice was worth the Squeeze

I could devote an entire chapter to just the trip itself. Scotland is a magical country with magnificent natural beauty and endlessly warm people. We welcomed blessings at every turn of the trip including smooth travel and sunshine. Occasionally I would wonder when I would have my "A-ha" moment when I would understand why I am here. But mostly, I lived in the moment. I soaked up every single experience in gratitude, which I understood later was ultimately the real lesson.

As I mentioned at the start of this chapter, I was offered a job to come work at the distillery doing health and safety, which I lovingly think of now as my "old life". How did that come about? Remember earlier how I mentioned that the ONLY day available to stay at the Glenmorangie House was Wednesday? It was for a good reason! As we drove to the House through the barley fields overlooking the blue waters of the Moray Firth, Eric commented that the area looked exactly as Dr. Bill described. Who?? I had literally never heard him mention a Dr. Bill before. He proceeds to tell me about the time he had a whisky tasting at

The Houstonian Hotel with Dr. Bill who just so happens to be the master distiller for Glenmorangie. I stared at him. Jeez babe! Didn't think to mention this sooner? "So THAT is why you wanted to come here?" I asked? He just shrugged as if it were completely obvious. He had no idea of the stress I put myself under while planning this. Yet, had I known this tiny but crucial piece of information, I would have had a completely different mindset about the whole process!

We reached the hotel grounds and pulled up to a fairly unassuming white stucco building. I am sure if that was the first building I had witnessed in Scotland, I might have been more impressed, but at this point, my eyes were nearly desensitized to all the incredible things we had seen so far. Looks can be deceiving! We entered the foyer, where we are immersed in an entirely new world, rich in texture and color. It was a feast for the senses. We were greeted by a lovely woman who regrettably informed us that she had some bad news. My heart dropped to the floor. There was a fleeting moment where I let myself think, ok so this is when the other shoe drops. She continued on to inform us that we will have several other guests joining us for dinner. "The master distiller and his leadership team are at the House for just tonight," she tells us. I laugh to myself. How hard I tried to not be here on this day, but it was meant to be!

We showered and dressed a bit nicer than we had initially planned since we knew we would be having dinner with some pretty important people later. The entire House had been recently renovated, and the four common spaces were cleverly created to represent one aspect of the whisky-making process. Our rare single-cask tasting was to be held at 6 PM in the drawing room. This room was done in a woodland motif to represent the importance of the cask and the flavor it imparts to the spirit. I learned so much during the private tasting, from the proper way to nose whiskey to how and why adding water changes the flavor and mouthfeel.

We were feeling pretty great after our four tastings. Now, it was time to move to the morning room for canapés and cocktails. The morning room was done up in brilliant hand painted gold to represent the sun and barley. This room was magnificent. As we approach the room, there is a mass of bodies in the doorway that we must navigate through. Immediately, a dark-haired man made a beeline for Eric and shook his hand. "I understand that we have met before." This is how I first met Dr. Bill.

Any fears or apprehension I felt going into the evening quickly dissipated. The team went above and beyond to include us in the conversation, and we felt as though we had all been friends for years. After cocktail hour, we were ushered into the dining room that is dripping in copper as a nod to the copper stills. I very consciously made my way to the end of the single table so that Eric and I would not be right smack dab in the middle of their dinner. It is so kind for them to include us, but surely dinner will be more for business, and we were mindful to not intrude. However, I had nothing to fear. The distillery manager sat across from me, and Dr. Bill sat across from Eric. And thus, began one of the most memorable dinners of my life. The stories, the wine, the food. Everything was perfection. At some point, it came up that the distillery manager would be taking on Health & Safety duties. I murmured my condolences. At his raised eyebrow, I went on to explain my experience in the area, and to my complete surprise, he asked if I wanted a job. I laughed it off, stating that I didn't know anything about their local laws to which he retorted, neither do I!

After dinner, all fourteen of us retired to the drawing room for more lively conversation and, of course, more whisky. I sat near Claire, the operations manager, and we clicked immediately. Slowly, people started to trickle out. I knew it must be late, but I didn't know the exact time. In the back of my mind, I kept thinking about the job. Was he serious? If I was having this much fun after just a few hours of meeting them, perhaps working with them would be equally fun and engaging. As I said goodnights and goodbyes to the distillery manager, I playfully joked that I will connect with him about the job. Claire overheard, and I explained what had happened earlier in the night. She looks me straight in the eye and says, "I would hire you in a heartbeat." I inwardly smiled as we headed to our room and got ready for bed. Even though it was 3 AM, and I was bone-tired, I was also giddy at the possibilities.

I must admit, it was very tempting. It felt good to be wanted, and the lure of a 'steady' paycheck had a real pull. Eric and I immediately started discussing what life could look like if we moved to Scotland. The opportunity to live in another country again was so enticing. I wasn't thrilled about "going backward" in accepting a position that I wouldn't truly love, but I was willing to sacrifice that for the bigger picture. It finally dawned on me that here I was again trying to control the situation. The absurdity of it actually made me laugh. Had I learned nothing? So I sat back and talked with God. I asked for clarity and guidance for my next best step. And then, I surrendered.

And wouldn't you know it? Once I had truly and utterly surrendered to God and allowed Him to work miracles on my behalf, He led me to my next point on the journey.

Ready for whatever comes next

Less than two weeks after we returned, I received a call from a networking friend, Anthony. He was ready to introduce me to his business partner. Anthony had been talking to me about his business partner for over six months, saying he was working on something big and felt like I could be a part of it. During all that time, Anthony never told me who his partner was or what the project was about. Apparently, I had finally learned the lesson, and God was ready to open the next door for me.

Anthony's business partner, Scott, was looking to create a meditation franchise and felt there was another person needed to make his dream a reality. He had a sense that this other person would be female. He didn't know until after he met Lacy and I that he was getting a two-fer! What we had spent the last year creating in Journey 2 Cloud 9 was a perfect fit for Scott's new business, Chill Meditation Centers. Scott knew it, and we knew it. He invited us to his home so that we could meet in person and be sure. The meeting went better than I could have imagined. It didn't dawn on me until much later that I was creating my new future on Scott's Land. Get it? The Universe has a great sense of humor!

The Grand Design

Looking back, I can see the whole design so clearly. The beauty of how each step forward (and sometimes step back) leads to the next opportunity and experience. This was the path that I needed to take to get me where I am today. I needed all of it.

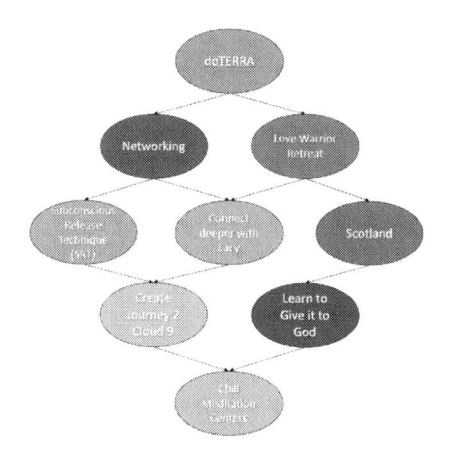

1. I needed to pursue doTERRA and believe in it so fully that I would take the steps to make it my main source of income. This started the process of opening my mind to the possibility that there is more available to me.
2. doTERRA placed me on the path that led me to attend the retreat and plant the seed to travel to Scotland.
3. Because of doTERRA, I was inspired to join networking groups, which led me to learning about SRT.
4. My desire to do more with SRT inspired me to reach a whole new level of friendship with Lacy that led to the creation of Journey 2 Cloud 9.
5. Traveling to Scotland helped to cement the lesson of relinquishing control and giving it to God.
6. Networking had put me on the path to connect with the right people.

DREAM, SURRENDER, THEN CREATE

The Lessons (so far)

- The most beautiful changes happen when I let go and give it up to God.
- The future is mine to dream and create and enjoy.
- It was never about the trip. It was who I became in preparation for the trip and in reflection afterwards.

To connect with Brianne, check out her amazing Etsy shop.

To learn more about SRT and how it can help, see if the Life Mastery program is right for you.

To see Scotland through my eyes, watch our highlight reel.

About the Author

CATRYN BECKER

Catryn began her mission to heal the planet in 2004 as an environmental engineer. Her career afforded her the opportunity to extensively travel the country as well as a few international trips to Australia, New Zealand, and the Philippines. In 2010, Catryn heeded the call to expand her knowledge by pursuing an MBA from a prestigious business school located in Milan, Italy. This allowed her to transition her career to management consulting in 2011.

After the birth of her second child, she felt called to take her life in a different direction. Catryn desired to affect change and transformation on the micro-scale in addition to the work she accomplished in consulting on the macro scale. She began studying alternative wellness modalities and healing techniques.

Catryn operates an online transformational coaching business called *Journey 2 Cloud 9* which focuses on business professionals and small business owners who are so overwhelmed and failing at balancing the responsibilities at work with their personal life. Her clients experience great results as her program is designed to align thoughts, feelings, and behaviors so that true, lasting transformation is achieved. She does this by utilizing the Subconscious Release Technique (SRT), Emotion Code, and Clifton Strengths in conjunction with other techniques as needed by each client's individual needs.

Catryn is excited to bring her knowledge, skills, and passions to her latest venture as CEO of Chill Meditation Centers, a franchise opportunity offering rest and relaxation to an overwhelmed world.

She lives outside of Houston, Texas with her husband and two children where they keep chickens, bees, llamas, and tortoises on their organic hobby farm.

Connect with Catryn:

On her website : www.journey2cloud9.com

Journey 2 Cloud 9 Facebook Group: www.facebook.com/groups/journey2cloud9

CHAPTER 4
Change of Heart – A Love Story

KIM TREMBLAY

My first impression of Hallie was when I went on a retreat with my work friends. She was very noticeable, quite loud, and a bit wild. Her laugh filled the large space, and me, being a huge introvert, just kind of looked at her with awe.

On that weekend back in February 2007, I had just been told that my husband of 17 years was leaving me. He said he just wasn't in love with me or happy anymore. He wanted something different in his life, which didn't include me. I didn't tell this to anyone on that weekend, keeping this to myself. I didn't want to take away from the weekend, which was all about First Nations Teachings along with a Moon Ceremony on the Saturday evening. I also knew I would likely lose it if I told anyone, and then it would be all about me, which, of course, would be very uncomfortable for me. I was in shock that weekend, keeping up appearances with a brave face, and just could not believe what had happened just hours before attending this event.

After that time, I dated a number of men, only to always feel disappointed. When it came to any kind of conflict or discussion around deeper issues, they just couldn't commit to working through them and would basically just run away. What I found was that the men were quite needy themselves and seemed to be looking for someone to save them. I went through a lot of heartbreak during that time. I was searching and yearning for a respectful, loving, and supportive relationship. I remember putting out an intention at one time that I wanted to meet a man who adored me. I did meet that man, but unfortunately, I didn't adore him back. Be careful what and how you wish for something. Right!

I did realize that it can be more challenging to find that perfect love when we all have our own life experiences behind us. I wanted to find that perfect, romantic love that would allow me to be my authentic self in a relationship. If I couldn't have that, I was truly okay with being single. I knew I was worth it and I was not going to settle.

The next time I met Hallie, it was early 2015 and she had just been hired as a Peer Support Worker working in Safety and Security with the women of My Sisters' Place, where I also worked. It is a mental health program that supports vulnerable women who are living on the streets, facing homelessness, mental health, and addiction issues, and/or living rough. When I saw her, I gave her a big hug, welcoming her. She was so friendly, and we would chat whenever we ran into each other.

It was July of 2015 when most of our staff decided to go out together on a Friday night. It was the opening night of the Pride Festival. We met up, had some food from the vendors, and had a couple of beers together while we chatted and watched the drag show. Hallie sat beside me, and she was so funny. She said, "let's pretend we are on a date and I will buy you a beer" with my ticket! She made me laugh so much. I left with another work friend that night, and I told her that I think Hallie has a crush on me. Ugh!

I had just ended it with someone a week earlier, so I was not thinking at all about jumping into something with someone else, especially not a woman. I mean, that thought had really not even crossed my mind. I had been married twice and had only ever dated men.

My Sisters' Place is a very busy place, but we continued to connect whenever we could, even if it was for a brief moment. That summer, we were planning a picnic for the women participants of My Sisters' Place, and Hallie asked if she could get a ride with me. Yes, of course, I picked her up and we just had a few laughs on the way there. Upon arriving at the picnic, we were still laughing, and I have a big laugh myself, so the two of us together were quite loud. The women there were all very quiet and just looking at us with that deer in the headlights look. Hallie can just get me laughing, and it brings out my crazy and fun side too.

Weeks later, after a long week, we agreed to go for a beer after work. We had an engaging conversation, some laughs, and some interesting moments. I dropped her off at her sister's place afterward, and as she was getting out of the car, she said to me, "to be continued." Ugh!! I was like, "No, this is not really happening." She sent me a text asking me if I wanted to continue the conversation, and there was no hesitation - it was a hard No.

When I got home, I really needed someone to talk to about what I was feeling. I got in touch with a friend who I could trust, and I expressed my thoughts around my emotions, my fears, and my doubts. She was able to calm me down and, of course, encouraged me to trust my heart. Maybe that was just what I needed to hear.

After a long quiet weekend of pondering, I decided to contact Hallie on Monday and ask her about the Moon Ceremony. She had mentioned it to me when we were together, and so I called her on Monday and told her that I wanted to go. I was no stranger to Moon Ceremonies in the First Nation Community as I had attended previously and have also been involved in Pagan Circles, so we also had that in common. We met up at the Moon Ceremony and I loved how she was with her community. Hallie was just so friendly and engaging with everyone, and of course, funny too. I was so enamored with her.

We continued to meet up as friends and we discussed what all of this might mean if we were to take it further, and, of course, the big question for me was "am I really up for this totally new way of living and ready for how others might react to this news". It was a big question, and I really didn't know. As time went on, though, the feelings were undeniably and obviously real.

We would run into each other at work and the emotions were charged, so we mostly tried to avoid each other. If we were in a meeting together, we avoided eye contact. Sometimes we would catch each other's eye and just be smiling at each other across the room. This would be among the chaos and drama of My Sisters' Place, which was always such a busy place. We really had to keep things on the down-low at work because we didn't know how things would play out. We were working with many vulnerable women every day, and we were just not ready for this to be a topic of conversation among clients or staff.

I have always been a very private person, somewhat of a people pleaser and wanting to be accepted by peers and especially family members. So the thought of others finding out I was with a woman felt very daunting to me. I really hated to upset the status quo. It was both a very exciting and scary time for me.

I remember just feeling so high, and I know that's what new love can feel like. I was with a group of friends one night and I was just bursting at the seams to tell them, but it just wasn't the right time. We were just new and unsure about what was unfolding and what it would all mean. We were both having a hard time keeping this secret.

We didn't really have a real date until the end of August 2015, when we went out for dinner and we actually held hands walking down the street, downtown of all places. A few days later, we went to the beach for the day, and after that, was when we started to tell people.

I wanted to tell my parents first. I often went shopping with my mom on Saturdays, so I really wanted to tell her and was quite nervous about it. Finally, just before we went into a shop, I told her and showed her a picture of Hallie. She could tell I was happy about it and seemed okay with it, and then she said, "I am not going to tell your dad". We went into the shop as if nothing had happened, and then I dropped my mom off at her home.

Later that night, I received a call from my mom saying she had told my dad and that he was fine with it. She said if you are happy, then we are happy and that's all that really matters. My parents loved Hallie. They told Hallie that she was the first date I had brought to their home to meet them, so they knew it must be serious. They could tell we were so happy together.

Once people started to find out, I am sure it was a surprise and there were some concerns. It was hard not to internalize some of those thoughts and messages into my heart and soul. I know that some people were just concerned about me and tried to understand and be supportive. I was getting messages like "Are you just exploring your sexuality?", "Is it serious?", "I don't think you should tell that family member", "Have you thought about what this person will think?", "I thought you said you wanted......", and questions about what assets she brought to the table?"

It felt hard not to hear those messages, and I really needed to process my own emotions and some doubts too. When I thought about the last eight years of my life and how unsuccessful I was in love and relationships, why would I think that this could work out?

The future is unknown, a mystery, and embracing love is a risk that we likely all take at some point. As I have gotten older and wiser, of course, I have less attachment to pleasing others and realize that we only live once, so why not spend the remaining time on this earth being as happy as possible? I knew that I needed to face the consequences of whatever was to happen. Most people have embraced our relationship and have commented on the fact that they have never seen me/us so happy.

Hallie has many beautiful gifts that she shares with all who love her. She has spiritual gifts, healing gifts, and musical talents to just name a few. She shares her wisdom openly and is so loved by everyone who knows her. She always comes from the heart, which is so wonderful to witness. I have learned so much from her and she definitely would say the same of me.

This is a song she wrote for me when we first met. It still brings tears to my eyes when I hear it, and I could listen to it over and over again.

When I look into your beautiful eyes,
I see something come to light in me.
When you took my hand that very first time,
My spirit never felt so free.
Now I know that dreams can really come true.
When you opened up your heart to me,
I just want to spend the rest of my life with you.
Giving you the best part of me
You'll never have to walk it alone.
You'll never have to face it alone.
You'll never have to walk it alone again,
Cause I am right where I belong.

I really never knew or felt love like this before. I finally feel like I am adored and loved for who I am. It feels so good. It really just happened out of the blue. It can really be true that once we stop the desperate search for love, then it just happens when we least expect it. Love is Love, my friends, and in the end, Love did win out. Our relationship is respectful and beautiful. She honors me for who I am and encourages me with whatever I want to do, never any judgment, just acceptance. She makes me want to be a better person. Of course, the feeling is mutual.

We always have fun together, go on some crazy adventures, and spend time at events like moon ceremonies, sweat lodges, Pow Wows, Pagan events, Women's Circles, Protests, Festivals, Markets - oh the list could go on and on. Hallie is always up for an adventure, and it's always a good day.

I have learned so much from Hallie, and I know she would say the same of me. We are just such a good fit together. Our personalities complement each other so much. She is quite outgoing, and I am more of a stay home on a Saturday night and watch Netflix kind of gal. I never used to be spontaneous, but now I find myself saying yes to things that come up at the last minute, and I embrace it and it works out great. I am so grateful and blessed to be able to experience the healing traditions and teachings of the First Nation Peoples. These would include but are not limited to smudging, giving thanks and prayers with tobacco, singing and dancing, healing circles, healing medicines, and braiding my partner's hair as I speak powerful words over her for her day.

It feels like the perfect love. Is our relationship perfect? Of course not, but it is perfect for us. Relationships are tough and are a lot of work. They are certainly not for the faint of heart. Yes, we have had our differences just like any couple, and I am sure we will have more. We have faced many challenges and differences together, but we always have been able to work through them and strengthen our relationship.

We have been together for seven years now, and we are still in love, still having fun, and living our best lives. Hallie is my best friend, my true love, and my soulmate, and I am so honored and proud to be the woman who walks beside her.

About the Author
KIM TREMBLAY

Kim Tremblay is a semi-retired mental health professional who is now following her lifelong passion as a Clutter Coach working with people to identify what is important in their lives by helping them to declutter both physical and emotional clutter. Kim helps people to create a home and a life that they love.

Kim Tremblay lives in London, Ontario with her partner and grandson. She's down-to-earth, a little rough around the edges, a self-help junkie with a positive attitude and never gives up. She is currently working on downsizing and simplifying her own life. Kim loves yoga, meditation, walking in nature, healthy food, and living an intentional and meaningful life.

In 2021, Kim debuted as a co-author in her first multi-author book collaboration, sharing her challenging story of hard beginnings and is back to share her positive success story of love in The Voyage & The Return.

Connect with Kim via:

Website | linktr.ee/KimberleyA

Facebook | www.facebook.com/KimSpaceForYou

Instagram | www.instagram.com/kimspaceforyou

CHAPTER 5

555 - A Story Of Faith, Resilience, And Change

JAMIE WAREHAM

555 in angel numbers means essentially, "hold on to your seat belts, major change is in progress." Ever since the night of February 19, 2011, when I see it, that number sequence sends a chill down my spine. You see, that was the night my mother, Debbie, unexpectedly passed away.

I had recently been introduced to Mary Jo McCallie, an Angel Therapy Practitioner in Tampa, Florida, and had begun working with her to start to understand some of my spiritual gifts. I had started to really work with the Angelic Realm and was in the process of building a communication channel with them, which included learning the angel numbers — one of the many ways the angels communicate messages to you.

On the evening of February 19, 2011, I received the number sequence "555" on a receipt after dinner and was excited by this new message from above. Little did I know that this message would reveal its darker meaning within just a few hours. On my way home from Orlando that evening, I received a call from my nephew, Joe, that my mom had just shockingly passed away. That was when my entire world changed. 555.

I spiraled down immediately after that night. I no longer cared about all the people and things that I once cared about so intensely. I call it my *Grand Reset*. A few years prior, I had a phoenix tattooed on my wrist to remind me that I will always have the power to rise again. Now, more than ever, I found myself staring down at my wrist — my phoenix. Depending on my Phoenix. For those of you who were there for me during this recreation process, I am and will be forever grateful. You helped me in ways you may never truly understand. I bless you for that.

This reset thrust me into working daily and diligently with the Archangels and the Spirit Realm. It also opened a Divine opportunity for me to meet my half-brother and my father's side of the family, who had also just happened to suffer a heartbreaking loss just two weeks before my own mother's death. Upon meeting, we both discovered our budding spiritual gifts and henceforth pursued them quite vigorously to help find our way to healing.

During that first year or two, I met souls who changed my life and are still with me to this day. As I mentioned previously, I started a private spiritual mentorship with Mary Jo (MJ) which is heavily focused on connecting to the Angelic Realms/Celestial Realms, discovering some of my gifts, and further developing my unique language with the other side. Learning all that I could about the angels and increasing my new ability to recognize and communicate with them helped me start to heal the gaping wound of my mother's death and that of my grandparents' passing just a couple of years prior. We were a very close family, so all these drastic changes impacted me immensely. It was a tough journey, hitting the breaks on my mental and emotional wheels that had spun out of control due to this series of life-altering changes that had occurred. What I did not know then was that the "life-altering" had only just begun. I continued my mentorship with MJ for years, assisting her in spiritual workshops, learning more and more about Angel Therapy and how to find peace and healing with this energy. I continued seeking and learning more outside of my mentorship work and delved deeper into the *magical* realms of working with the angels as well as further studies into various spiritual cultures around the world. I started to draw connections between the many magical and esoteric practices and rituals. I began to see the big picture of the Universe and how it builds a blueprint for each soul's journey. I saw how our human hearts, with all their collected traumas (blocks, fears, ego-mind, etc.), and losses are really all a part of a spiritual puzzle. Our *Soul Contracts* determine our journey, to an extent, and there is truly no controlling or planning that can stop a path that is meant to unfold. We cannot save people; we can only plant seeds so that they can save themselves.

"You cannot stop a train wreck."

That line sticks with me to this day. A dear friend, Kim Truitt, delivered that message to me during a séance I had been invited to. She unintentionally channeled that message from my mother that night regarding my sister, Wendy. You see, I had been invited to simply bring the Angelic protection energies and to hold space at this mediumship séance session. However, when my mom wants attention, she gets attention. Mom actually pushed through with a few messages for me, mostly regarding my sister Wendy.

Mom, the party crasher!

Now, let me step back a couple of years from the night of the séance. After I had connected with my brother and we both began our spiritual transformations of healing, within months he took me to a magical little metaphysical shop in Dunedin, Florida, called Enchanted Earth. It was just a few miles away from my house, which turned out to be a wonderful bonus as years went by. He introduced me to the shop owner, Kim Truitt. I was very shy and quiet, simply taking it all in. Something felt different about that place, though, and I had no idea how important it would soon become.

Between Angels Talk and Enchanted Earth, I have been blessed with more connections and healing moments than I could ever have imagined.

In tandem with my mentorship with Angels Talk, I started hanging out at the shop and taking various spiritual courses ranging from Celtic studies to scrying. I met interesting people along the way, both those that worked at the shop as well as customers having coffee or tea and exchanging stories about their spiritual explorations. It became not only a shop to purchase supplies and learn new intuitive modalities, but a little magical community. I became quite close with some of the people there, and they, too, helped me heal in different ways.

Unexpected ways.

Kim became like a sister to me, and my brother was able to hone his spiritual gifts and became a professional Tarot reader at the shop.

Life was changing before my eyes and in a very magical way.

During this time, my sister had been struggling in ways that I did not know how to effectively help with. Both in our own painful places due to these losses so close to our hearts and her worsening medical challenges, we felt very disconnected. I was broken. I had trouble forgiving things that had happened, and I just wanted everything to go back to how it was before it all seemed to fall apart, but it wouldn't, it couldn't. We were both dealing with levels of pain that neither of us could help with. The distance grew. We would sometimes get into verbal fights and not talk for months at a time, and then mend our emotional differences and try again. We did have some great times though, funny times, that I will remember in my heart forever. When we laughed together, it was contagious. However, so much was broken in us with no real road map to healing it. I called on my angels and my mom for help. They helped me on my journey, but apparently, it was not my course here to help my sister get better. Less than a year before her death in a heart-to-heart conversation during one of her hospital visits, she had said to me that she had always been "broken" and that she "was done trying to feel" and that she "couldn't be fixed" and was of no use here. Now, let me be clear, this was just one of her moments of depression, and this was not meant as a warning. For the record, she had no intention of passing away.

It broke my heart.

The painful and sudden loss of my sister Wendy on August 1, 2018, due to an accidental prescription fentanyl overdose, launched me further into my own personal quagmire of shadow work and forgiveness.

I had already lost one of my oldest and closest friends in 2015 to a drug overdose, and now my world was being rocked again.

I was numb.

Our family core was small in comparison to many other families, and after having lost both my grandparents, who were our rocks, and the shock of losing my mother to things I had felt could have been prevented, to losing my oldest best friend to an overdose, and then losing my sister to an accidental prescription fentanyl overdose... well, the strands of the life I once knew had faded into oblivion.

My aunt and uncle, while in Maine, have been and continue to be my rocks, the embodiment of kindness and my connections to all the memories of the past. Wendy's boys, my two nephews, still live near me, but I don't tend to see them much. With my oldest nephew, Joe, sometimes I think the pain of all our losses gets in the way of more time spent together. So much left to heal. As for my youngest nephew, Anth, he seems to somewhat favor his solitude. I suppose everyone heals (or doesn't) in their own unique way with family loss.

Joe was the one who called me when my mom, Debbie, died — he found her. Anthony was the one who called me when Wendy died — he found her.

So much pain still exists.

When I got the call that my sister had accidentally overdosed, I went numb. It was an entirely different feeling than when my mom passed.

Maybe, I had hit my emotional limit?

I know, I quite frankly yelled out to the Universe that I had hit my absolute limit. I went into somewhat of a robot mode to deal with what needed to be done and all the processes that, I felt, fell on my shoulders. When my mother passed, I had the help of close friends who assisted in what had to be sorted, settled, planned, and organized. However, this time I felt I had no room to grieve. I was the eldest one left now in Florida to take care of the aftermath of this latest heartbreak. I was the eldest left and couldn't stop thinking about what "the boys" were going to do. Mind you, "the boys" were fully grown adults, but my brain just wasn't registering things properly. This culmination of painful losses was just too much for me to take. Even though I had already become a healer, a practitioner, a reader, and a spiritual teacher, this weight was so heavy. It was just too much.

With that said, having endured multiple traumas, even from a young age, my knee-jerk reaction to extreme emotional pain is *survival mode*. This spiritually-centered version of me, the healer and teacher, knows very well that this is an unhealthy mode to spend too much time in. My inner child, however, also knew that it got *her* through some of the painful situations thus far.

Inner child for the win.

I wanted to break down, fall apart, grieve... but I couldn't. My body and emotions wouldn't cooperate. I was numb. Not because I didn't care, Lord no. I was devastated. Another piece of me was gone. First my mother, then my sister. No matter how complicated my relationship with Wendy was, I loved her very much.

I forgave her.

Some time had gone by, but I was still in robot mode, and I was starting to get worried. I said to myself, "I think something's wrong. Why haven't I broken down yet?" It's as if Wendy had heard me at that moment. The next day, I felt the Spirit tell me to play our local 70s rock station. You see, ever since I can remember, music has always been one of our bonds. She used to quiz me on Pink Floyd, Lynyrd Skynyrd, etc. Anyway, I put the station on and immediately the song "Simple Man" came on the radio. I looked directly at the sky and began uncontrollably crying and talking to her, releasing all that had been trapped inside me. For some reason, I was absolutely compelled to tell her how sorry I was. Sorry that we butted heads our entire lives together, sorry for staying mad instead of seeing the true pain that had caused her to act in ways that she did. Sorry for losing the time we could have had together.

So many "sorries".

She comes to visit me sometimes. My spiritual journey has taught me skills and how I can better communicate with her even on the other side. For this, I am eternally grateful. A powerful bolt of lightning hit my house just seven days before Wendy's overdose. It's as if the Gods were sending an electrifyingly shocking warning that something huge was coming – 555.

Her last text to me said, "Things can be replaced – You Cannot. Major halos!!"

While all this heartbreak ripped open my world, it was also very transformative and has guided me in following the path that the Universe has laid out for me. Directing me to be present more fully in my purpose. All this emotional destruction helped me see who I truly was and am becoming. The shy, people-pleasing, "fixer" has become something more. Something stronger. Something with purpose. After that loss, I continued to dive even deeper into the spiritual world as well as the personal transformation studies such as: Life Coaching, NLP, Access Consciousness techniques, deep dives into reclaiming self-worth, shadow work for transformation, clearing energetic blocks due to past traumas, and turning "triggers" into keys to set you free. I teach these things now. Some of the best teachers are ones who have journeyed into the *heart of darkness* and come through it all like the powerful Phoenix they are! A rebirth into something else, something stronger, something that yearns to help others through their own forms of darkness.

We are Phoenix.

This was a piece of my story on healing. A chapter in my journey and path to rediscovery. My 555.

About the Author
JAMIE WAREHAM

Jamie Wareham has been working with the Ascension Realms for over a decade. She is a Certified Angel Intuitive Practitioner, Shamanic and Usui Reiki Master Teacher, Psychic Reader, Life Coach, and Sound Healing Practitioner.

Jamie is the founder of LightworkerPath.com and co-facilitator at AngelsTalk.com. Her passion is helping others awaken to their Divine Paths through intuitive development, working with the Angels, meditation, Western magical practices, energy healing, NLP, and coaching techniques. Being a natural Clairsentient, she has empathy for those just opening-up to these new energies and, after facilitating over 1,500 healings, has a unique ability to bring ease and comfort during her sessions with individuals. Jamie also provides group classes on topics ranging from Angel Magic to energy medicine techniques. She also has online study courses and offers both in-person and online Healings/Readings, Spiritual Mentorships, and Life Coaching Sessions.

Find out more about Jamie by visiting her website: www.LightworkerPath.com

CHAPTER 6
Total Life Reboot
CAROLINE BENGTSON

The room felt so sterile, so cold, and so terrifying. It was June 12, 2012. I remember the day like it was yesterday. I was alone in the exam room of a world-renowned surgeon, James Reynolds. I felt he held my life in his hands. Well, at least my ability to walk. There were tears leaking out of my eyes, tears of grief, fear, and abandonment.

His office was in San Francisco. I had just made a long trip during a difficult time and had been unable to change my appointment because I was a workers compensation patient. Those were the rules. I'd flown home the day before and was here waiting to meet him. So much pain, not only physically, but now emotionally and mentally as well. I felt alone, vulnerable, and scared. Just three days prior, my beloved momma had passed. I was in Edmonton, Alberta at her bedside for the previous month and on Saturday June 9th, at 2:30AM, she took her last breath. She was all I had, or so it seemed. I was now an orphan. My relationship with my siblings was strained at best, and we were not especially close. We'd grown up under very difficult circumstances. It was each one for themselves.

Still, even though I wanted to, I was unable to stay with my family for even one extra day. The waves of grief washed over me, and this was on top of the incredible levels of physical pain I was experiencing.

How could this be happening? It couldn't be real? Or was it? So surreal. Life had been so good, almost perfect a year ago. I had started what I thought was my dream job in 2010, a few short months after my dearest Bichon, Mili, had crossed the Rainbow Bridge. I was working for a big international B2B sales company, lived on the coast just south of San Francisco, and had secured a cute two-bedroom house to rent at a great price. I could even see the ocean from my house, and it was only three blocks to the beach. And there is more. Not only was I living in one of the prettiest areas of my life, I had a large circle of people who gathered every weekend for live music and dancing; I spent much time with an intimate group of friends for barbecues and happy hour, and I was actively dating. My life seemed complete, so much fun. What I didn't foresee was a tragic event that would change everything.

It was August 31, 2010. I got up and went to work like any other day. Happy and on top of the world as I spent much of my day outside walking and meeting with business owners. My clients included everyone from a small car repair shop to eBay. Little did I know, this was the day my life would change forever. I loved asking on any given day, "Who will I meet today?" Sales is my love. Having studied accounting in college decades earlier, that career was short-lived. I loved to be free, to meet people and enjoy the outdoors. My love of people was what had prompted me in the mid 90s to create a company with toys and gifts and teaching materials. It was fun and had the diversity of activities to keep my attention. This work was my love for years as I built the company to three-quarters of a million dollars in sales. An insatiable desire to meet people and learn about them was the drive behind my love of sales. The freedom to be outside, meeting a diverse clientele, and providing a much-needed service were all factors in my high level of job satisfaction. Truly, this was my element.

The day began just like every other day. Looking at my sales territory, my job was going to take me to the warehouse district of San Francisco. It had been fertile ground for me in the past. With deadlines to meet, I smiled happy this was where I was headed. It was a beautiful sunny day. I was excited to visit amazing organic wholesalers with products I had never seen before, as well as many other great companies and food purveyors. I was in my glory. At about 3:30PM, I walked up a few stairs to a cleaning business. The door was locked. I remember coming back down the stairs and failing to notice the platform at the bottom was in disrepair. Moving quickly as the day was coming to a close, and realizing I had not secured a deal yet, I remember stepping down with my right foot. At the same time, my left foot was coming up, the platform below my right foot gave way. My right heel was caught in the wooden pallet, and my body kept moving forward. It was like in slow motion as my binder and presentation materials that I was carrying flew out of my hands. I crashed down on my hands and knees. Ouch!

Stunned and on all fours, my first reaction was complete embarrassment. I looked around to see if anyone had witnessed my fall from grace. Nope, thinking, "whew, okay, get up and dust yourself off and get out of here." My heart was racing as I stood up. There was a noticeable pain in my back, and I was limping. No visible signs of the fall, no ripped pants, so I literally wiped myself off and scurried to my car to get out of there as quickly as I could. Dear gawd, looking back, I'm wondering why I felt such shame that this had occurred. Shame that there was a rotten step? What was that all about?

My car was close, and I was grateful because I was hurt. I drove down the street to an underpass to collect myself and my thoughts. Totally not a safe area of town, and it just didn't matter. My heart was still racing as I leaned my head back and closed my eyes for a few minutes. Buzz buzz, it's my phone. I opened my eyes and realized it was my boss checking on me. We had a conversation and, not wanting to create problems, I only casually mentioned that I had fallen and hurt myself. There was nothing on my radar reminding me to properly detail and report an injury, and she didn't ask for anything beyond surface questions. The ramifications of this vague exchange escaped me and would later come back to haunt me.

It would be many more years before I would understand what was underneath my lifelong wish to be invisible, to go with the flow and not cause any problems for others. It was another decade before I understood that it gets complicated when we seek to live a life of not causing waves, of trying to fit into the norm, of hiding and being invisible. A childhood of trauma, neglect, and abuse translated into being seen and then running for cover, and a system of self-sabotage that was almost impenetrable, which would result in many complications and disappointment in the years to come. This was the start of "The Journey and The Return."

The next four years were hell on earth. There is not one moment of that time that I would wish on anyone. It was pure torture. Delays and more delays and more delays to the point that there were four major surgeries where there could have been only two!

Not to dwell on the pain, yet to fully understand, it's important to know what the surgeries were. First was my back fusion. It was a six-hour surgery where the lower three vertebrae were fused and a cage was installed in my back for stability. The good news, as my surgeon pointed out to me, is that I could probably fall out of a second-story window and be okay. I was thinking, "Whoever plans to fall out of a second-story window?" Somehow, that was not terribly comforting. This was the most complicated of my surgeries, and it took place the day before Thanksgiving 2012. My doctors could see my declining mental state due to my pain levels and, rather than postponing until after the holidays, moved ahead to bring hope to me. Up until that point, it was still believed that my pain was solely radiating from my back. Just weeks before my surgery, it was discovered that the second layer of extreme pain was due to my left hip deteriorating due to the fall. There had been complete wear on my hip joint. By seeing only a back specialist a total injury prognosis was missed. There was more to my fall than I initially thought. The hip damage had not been discovered due to the fact that I was seeing a back surgeon, and until surgery was scheduled, there were simply x-rays of my back to go by. The hip problem was missed. We were shocked.

The day before Thanksgiving 2012 was the six-hour surgery. There were complications and a spinal leak, so I was being closely watched. The hospital staff were not careful enough, and one day after surgery, as they were getting me up on my feet, I fell over and landed on the floor. It was a mess.

A few days later, I was transferred to a rehabilitation hospital and, "hallelujah," the only room available was a private room with an ocean view. Hope! My surgeon, knowing that my mental state was bleak, had arranged for an amazing therapist to come visit me to begin processing the changes in my life. It was six weeks before I was released from the facility. That year, I spent Thanksgiving, Christmas, and New Year's in a hospital. It took that long to get treatment for the spinal leak, and the daily headaches were unbearable.

There were so many twists and turns in the Voyage. Both of my hips were replaced, and I had bilateral sacroiliac joint surgeries. I've joked over the years that I am probably worth more for parts than anything else. This was a long and arduous Voyage, and it was further complicated by the injustices I endured, the agony, and the feelings of worthlessness as I struggled and clawed to receive the care I needed. There was so much incompetence, especially on behalf of my legal team. How can so many lawyers drop that many balls? A six-million-dollar lawsuit was lost because head counsel was on another case and a junior was assigned to me. My surgeon was shocked, as his testimony alone should have been enough to win the case.

These occurrences further fed the "victim" who was running my subconscious mind. TM

My daily thoughts involved looking under every rock in my life to try to understand what I had done so wrong to deserve this situation. I looked at Karma. I looked at anything I had ever done wrong in my life. I truly believed that this was all my fault. I was being punished and for what? I've tried to live a good life. Nothing at this point was making any sense. I continued to spin in the questions of "how I got here and what had I done to deserve this. " A futile conversation, I might add.

This was a crash course in survival skills. My mental state continued to decline with the added isolation from not being able to walk. There were days I crawled to the bathroom, as had happened at my sister's before my mom passed. The pain was level 10 every moment of every day. It felt like I was going crazy. I was certainly feeling bitter, hopeless, and suicidal.

The final surgery was in February 2014. The next two years are to hurry up and wait before we would have a final determination of my level of disability. My case took much longer because of all the complications, and in 2017, there were additional factors to consider.

The turning point of the Journey

December 2017 was a pivotal time in my life of doing a life reflection, feeling the continued hopelessness of chronic pain, and having goodbye conversations with close friends. It was my desire for people to know I knew they loved me. My choices were simply that I could not live another 10-20 years like this. I felt it was a hopeless existence every day. Even with an amazing friend I'd met the previous year, life was lonely, painful, and not worth living. What lay ahead on April 21st, 2018, was my 60th birthday. I had not been able to find a way off this planet, and it occurred to me that I had at least 20 plus more years on this earth. "Oh, dear gawd."

And then, the spirit spoke to me. This power rose in me, and with my right hand, I virtually drove a stake in the ground and yelled, **"NO!!! This is NOT going to be my life."**

2018 was the turning point. I declared to the spirit that things were going to change, and guess what? Resources, ideas, and options began to present themselves; I found a part-time job that gave me financial freedom to do more with my days. I discovered hot yoga. And every time I stood on one leg, I fell over. Nonetheless, that led me to Yin Yoga, and after three months, my legs seemed stronger. I declared that next year, when my niece and I went to Hawaii, I would get out of the water on my own instead of being a turtle on my back with my arms and legs flailing waiting to be rescued. In December 2018, I found a small ad for a "Vision Workshop" thinking it was a vision board workshop, I paid my money and signed up.It wasn't. Attending the workshop was terrifying. When I arrived, it was quickly apparent that this was not a vision board class. I almost bolted.. My little voice reminded me, "I had paid for this, so I should stay."

The next 3 hours changed the course of my life. I'm so happy I listened to my little voice. I knew what this lady was talking about: a ten-step process of transformation that would actually work. I signed up for a call with her and started coaching with her a couple of weeks later.

Thus began my Return!

2022 and wow, I am sitting here on my lanai (balcony) in Waikiki, Hawaii and honestly, I am in awe of who I am and the Return to me. Had it not been for everything during those years, my evolution would not have been the same. I am a successful Transformational Life and Leadership Coach; I am a TranscenDanceTM Facilitator. I work with individuals and teams of students, standing for a transformed world. My summits continue to grow. I have reached countries and continents all over this world. None of this would have transpired without my fall on August 31st, 2010. Would I wish those years on anyone? NO! Would I change who I have become in the process? NO!

Today I live a life of gratitude, for everything and in everything. When I look at the circumstances in my life, I get curious about how and why I am creating this. I work with some of the most amazing leaders in the world. My life has more impact than I could have ever imagined.

The return to Caroline has been nothing short of miraculous.

If you find yourself with circumstances that feel like a tidal wave of destruction hitting your life, I encourage you to know that this too shall pass. We all have circumstances, and it does no good to compare ourselves to others. Comparison is the thief of JOY! I know that there is good in everything, even a traumatic childhood. The word "why" is one of the most disempowering words in the English language and has been banished from my life. And lastly, you are more than your circumstances.

Looking back to 2012, what would I tell Caroline?

What do I know for sure?

Life is a series of choices. We create our own reality, no one else's. I am 100% responsible for everything in my life, past, present, and future. Had I not had a traumatic childhood, I would not be able to identify a trauma response in my students and clients. I am the creator of my life and everything in it is here to serve me. Even my difficult childhood, the six car accidents I've survived, and the four major surgeries I've "endured" have brought me to this amazing place. I've allowed the conditions to teach me, to see how I have sourced each and every occurrence in my life. I have learned empathy, kindness, patience, trust and surrender. Coming home to me would not have occurred without August 31st, 2010. Today I am simply grateful.

What else have I learned? I am more than I ever believed I was. I have more love in my life, more joy in my life, and more power in my life. I am a leader in supporting people in Transforming their lives.

In December 2019, Dr. James Reynolds retired. He and his wife were going to be giving their time to the Walnut Creek, California food bank. Although it had been over a year since I'd seen him last, I booked one of his last appointments. As he entered the same exam room where we had met over 7 years prior, his face lit up like a Christmas tree. In the year since I had seen him, I had released over 70 pounds. I had completed my Life Coaches Training and was full of life and stories of goodness. We hugged, and I cried. What was my message to him that day? All the love and care he had poured into me was noted and appreciated. I knew that I would continue to build an amazing life because he had so generously poured into my body, mind, and spirit, and I was so grateful to him.

His response, with tears filling his eyes, was the most loving words I had ever heard; "You are the person I have waited my entire career to meet!"

Circumstances. We all have them. My question that begs answering is, "what will you create beyond your circumstances?"

About the Author

CAROLINE BENGTSON

Caroline Bengtson is a certified Life Mastery Consultant, Transcendence Facilitator, and Chief Abundance Officer of Push Your Paradigm, a Transformational Coaching and Speaking company located in Honolulu, Hawaii.

Caroline is a sought-after summit speaker and host, featuring speakers from all over the globe. Caroline has studied and practiced transformation for over 30 years, understanding the principles of focus, manifesting and embodying the life we are designed to live.

Through many trials and health challenges that resulted in a diagnosis of permanent disability Caroline continued to achieve, and surpass the norm, to live beyond the diagnosis. In 2018, weighing in at 254 pounds, requiring a cane to walk around the block, and living in chronic pain, Caroline began to rebuild through her vision, utilizing decades of health study and working with a coach. She has survived 6 car accidents, and a fall that resulted in four major surgeries and truly embodies resilience and resourcefulness in her life. Through her darkest hours, Caroline continued to give through fostering and saving over 20 pups that would have been destroyed through no fault of their own. Because giving is at the core of her being Caroline also coaches leadership programs with some of the world's foremost trainers.

Inspiring her clients who feel like they are stuck and have no hope, to rebuild and create a life they would truly love is one of Caroline's superpowers. She is often overheard asking the question, "What would you love?" We truly can and do create our lives through our thoughts, actions, words, and visions.

Caroline has a ten-step transformational process and designs a system for structure and accountability to ensure her clients achieve the results they are looking for in their lives. Caroline embodies what it means to live a life you love. In 2021 after repeatedly stating she wanted to move to Hawaii, Caroline created the move in three short months. Anything is possible with a system of support, accountability, and a clear vision.

What is your Hawaii? What would you love? What are you going to create with your one precious life?

Connect with Caroline:

On Facebook: www.facebook.com/caroline.bengtson

On Instagram: www.instagram.com/pushyourparadigm

Website: www.pushyourparadigm.com

CHAPTER 7
Trusting My Inner Knowing
APRIL AZZOLINO

I find a lot of people have self-doubt. Being influenced by the structures of society or believing in what family or friends tell them what they need to do for themselves. Trusting my inner senses may seem like moving against what society says I need to do for myself, yet those inner senses of knowing, vision, hearing, and feeling will be my guidepost.

When I was ten years old, in fifth grade, my twin sister and I decided to try out to be cheerleaders. We never asked our parents if we could. We were already free thinkers by then. I will give credit to my parents. They didn't realize they were creating daughters who were making decisions for themselves on their own. We went home and told our parents we made the cheerleading squad and they needed to fork over some money. We needed cheerleading outfits and to be dropped off and picked up from basketball games, plus cheerleading practice.

Imagine the look on their faces. This was the 70's. My parents trusted us to walk home from school by ourselves while they had jobs to be at. We had a secret key to get into the house. By then, we had been dutifully taught to clean the house and cook something for ourselves. I believe this was the beginning of trusting that inner knowing of my senses.

By the time I got to high school, I didn't always trust my inner knower. I went along with the crowd on more than one occasion. Then those occasions had a consequence to pay afterward. Lessons learned about what was not working for me.

At 19 years old, I left my Kentucky home and moved to Florida with a boyfriend. He wanted to get married. My inner knower said, "no" Thank goodness I listened. He was a fine mess of a country boy. Divorce court would have seen us both. Passing my twenty-third birthday, I fell madly in love with another boyfriend who lived in Germany and was a Turkish Muslim. Contrary to my Christian upbringing, my inner knower knew we were too different, and as luck would have it, he broke up with me.

I had at this time left attending a community college because I understood I wasn't going to live a traditional life of college, marriage, and kids. I instead enrolled in Beauty School, where I got to play with my unique, creative senses. Trusting myself that I was capable of living my own style of life. I lived in South Florida on my own. I had many roommates come and go in my apartments. I never asked my parents for a hand-out. All though looking back, I could have used some extra dollars.

The marriage finally happened at forty-one. We had ten years of dating each other on and off. My inner knowing just knew it was finally right to say, "I Do." And we did. Along the journey, I left my comb and scissors for a new love. Thirty-one years later, the small still voice inside my head said it was time to quit the hair profession. The energy wasn't there anymore. Trusting what was next for me, but I wasn't quite sure.

I mean, I am not exactly the Betty Crocker kind of gal. Except I do love to cook a great meal.

Just before I left the beauty biz, a client introduced me to my next career —Spiritual Mentoring.

It was the inner hunch of trusting myself. Leaving behind a career of over thirty years to begin a new and different journey. In helping people find their beauty within instead of the beauty of the physical body they paid me for. Both are important, but soul beauty will last from lifetime to lifetime. So I began investing in my own soul beauty because I know I will take that with me when I leave this planet. I will not be able to take my hair or my make-up bag.

Except I was so skeptical.

Will I have the confidence, courage, and ability to be of service in this way? I needed to explore my why more. What I found. People are really hungry for spiritual growth and more today than ever. Discovering myself was an essential need. Exploring my own psychic sensitivity, communicating with my inner guidance/angels, and trusting my soul nature. Living inside a body as a soul can have its challenges. I began the journey to really trust all of myself, every day. Trusting my sensitivity became an investment. A spiritual investment of my soul.

We all need spiritual mentors in this game of life. I, too, searched for those who can help me along my path to living fulfilled and happy. My mentor helped me understand my own psychic sensitivity, higher guidance, and living in two worlds at once through the programs of New Spiritual Horizons, a department of Wayshowers College. A spiritual development school of learning through experience. I have personally grown more in one week by this personal choice. I feel grateful I took action on my feelings. The payoff is I am more secure, confident, and live my own personal freedoms daily.

I have gained more in this lifetime than I thought was possible. Sometimes it is just about putting one foot in front of the other. I had no idea where I was going, but I knew my higher wisdom was sending me messages to follow along. Staying curious. Allowing my inner guidance to show the way. I learned to ask better questions to myself; such as, What am I focusing on today? In what way will this benefit me and the individuals who seek what I have to offer? The better the questions I present to myself, the better the answers seem to come, knowingly.

It's been 14 years since I began my inner voyage of self-discovery. I am now 58, closing in on 60 soon. Following a path that wasn't common or even talked about as much then as it is now. That mystical part of all of us. I have taught online classes and live classes by returning to what I know to be true for my soul. Guiding others on their own self-discovery journey.

Along the way, I became certified as a hypnotist. At first, when I decided to study this healing modality, I doubted myself. Then I became curious about Past Life Soul Regression work for soul healing. It truly is marvelous to be able to guide someone into a past life and find healing of karmic issues or patterns. I have found out for myself that when I am in the zone of trusting my innate wisdom, it is like a lighthouse always shining me to my inner home of who I am. I also guide individuals in discovering methods for angel communication. Both private sessions are just the beginning of a path of finding one's own inner beauty of the soul. I am delighted I chose to follow my heart. It has led me down unknown roads with people in other countries and new friends.

What I have learned so far is that my fifth-grade cheerleader is still inside myself. Cheering me on to hear without ears, see without eyes, feel without a touch, and trust my hunches. Those inner communication pathways that reside in all of us. When I do that, I am living my truest dreams of living on this planet.

This planet is a self-discovery planet for the soul. Each time I return back on a new voyage, I spiral into a greater expansion of my energy. It is the beauty of being here.

What lies ahead on the voyage? Who knows! Now I live trusting more every day working with my inner guidance so that I am always returning to the real me on this spiritual voyage called life.

About the Author
APRIL AZZOLINO

April Azzolino, International Spiritual Mentor/Past Life Soul Regression Specialist living in Las Vegas, Nevada. She was recently published in *Breathe magazine* Vol. #42 about her insights in the seven year cycles of life.

She is pioneering modern methods in the field of Spiritual Development, Intuitive & Angel Communication. April started her own journey by following an inner hunch after being introduced to New Spiritual Horizons, a department of the Wayshowers College. She has gained an understanding of her spiritual gifts and natural abilities as a highly sensitive soul.

April is enthusiastic, authentic, and boldly funny in a way that helps us to create our true heart's desire. Her uncanny abilities help us see that living a practical spiritual life is easy.

April's passion is facilitating Angel Communications Sessions and Past Life Soul Regressions. April assists others in connecting with their own spiritual team of guides. Releasing incarnated karmic patterns of the past to living more free.

Connect with April on her website: www.aprilazzolino.com

CHAPTER 8

Connecting to the Voice of our Soul

TARA CAMPBELL

The first time I slept in a jungle by myself, I became witness to new sensory perceptions that were beyond my current experiences. The rustling of distant leaves and the scurry of an insect beneath the house made my vulnerable awareness very clear of the known and unknown presences outside the four walls of my *cabana*. There was a power, vibrancy, and force in the jungle that held spaces and had incomprehensible voices that intrigued me. I could feel so much was alive. It was also a time I remember connecting with an inner strength I didn't know I had due to the uncertainty of what could appear in the expanse of this nocturnal tropical wilderness. These spaces from the density of the forest were calling to me with a voice I was hearing for the first time, and I was listening. Throughout my life, I have been inspired by many journeys like this one, calling me with their distinct voices and guiding my path of self-discovery.

Ever since I can remember, I have been referred to as a highly sensitive person or as being 'different.' I have heard voices in unknown spaces, knew something before it happened, felt things that others couldn't feel, and at times, it has been uncomfortable. However, despite this feeling of being different, I have come to accept my divine essence as the unique energetic blueprint of my individuality. Perhaps it was this difference that set me on the path of being an educator, leader and eventually a healer where I utilized this sensitivity as my strength.

Healing has always been a part of my life. I began yoga at a young age when I experienced a tragedy with the sudden passing of my mother at nineteen. Yoga in Sanskrit means "to unite" and connects the body, mind, and spirit. The practice of this internal connection to the divine, at a time when it was hardly popular decades ago, gave me early training to access deep states of soul-based introspection and would be my foundation for most of my life. My mother was my closest friend and ally, and this incredible loss had set me on the path of having to emotionally support myself, and I felt broken. I would practice yoga postures in my room for hours, balancing my nervous system to calm my breath to be able to greet the next day. This grief caused me to feel alienated in many ways, and I became connected to this grief. I embodied the belief that I could be tied to my mother forever in the ethers with it, and I wanted to hold on tight. This ethereal cord connected my inner voice and knowing to the outside world and became a catalyst for my self-awareness.

It takes only one journey to change your life forever, and for me, it was a trip to India. Stepping off the plane in this diverse country where the fragility of life seems so apparent immediately made me feel at home. The sights, sounds, and richness of India made daily experiences precious and the serendipity of what could happen created events of momentous delight. Every day, I felt the essence of thousands of lifetimes in the dense activity of city streets, and I would sip in the sensory overload of an ancient civilization when drinking chai from the local street corner. I was part of a group from a Canadian university for a semester of living with a local family in Jaipur, Rajasthan. Being welcomed into this Indian family, I was treated as a daughter where days were spent at university and evenings at home sharing stories with my new sister, also of the same age. We laughed, talked, found comfort in our familiarity beyond cultural differences, and connected our global timelines. India had undoubtedly welcomed me into her calling, and I experienced my soul's expansion and connection to new lands.

When I returned to Canada, the calling of distant voices from stories of continents across the world tempted me, and I next found myself on a small island in Japan. Aside from my local bicycle, adventures included visits to Buddhist temples, cherry blossom festivals, and karaoke-filled weekends. I spent mornings studying calligraphy with a Zen master and practicing the strategy of meditation for stillness and flow that permeated my green tea-infused days of teaching English on a one-year contract at a local school. The experience in this foreign land brought me closer to my sensory evolution. However, there was more ahead on my return than I could have anticipated.

Returning home, I was faced with another tragedy that would yet again shake my foundations. When I received the news that my father would pass away from a terminal illness within a year after my arrival, I lost my second parent before the age of thirty. It was a difficult time, and I did my best to move forward with the grace that only time would heal. My expansion into the ethers grew deeper with the experience of grief and loss of my father and, with it, a tighter grip of having to emotionally support myself. Within a year after my father's passing, the familiar call of distant lands had reached out to me, and I next traveled to the jungles of Costa Rica for fieldwork for a Masters degree. I was content in the natural world, finding solace in the spaces between healing plant energies and developing environmental education programs around the sensory experience of medicinal plants.

My connectedness to the ethereal realms continued to expand in ways I was not always able to comprehend. The practice of yoga was still part of my firm foundation over the years, and while my intentional awareness of divine spaces grew, I was soon to find out it would develop with random experiences too. Shortly after my return from Costa Rica, when I was in a meditation session at home with a friend, a sudden and profound energetic activation occurred in my body and consciousness. This sudden shift was quite destabilizing, and little did I know it would affect me for years and decades afterward. Since this experience, I have become more aware of the quantum field and, with clearer perception, I realized these shifts in consciousness and associated experiences would have a purpose for me later in life. Meanwhile, I felt it best to try and forget the impact these experiences had on me at the time and avoid accessing spiritual realms I was uncertain of, and that is what I did.

The next journey that called to me months later would fill my world with the language of Spanish and Portuguese. My life shifted to South America for a one-year contract as an adventure tour leader that became almost a decade full of tales of wonder. The thrilling hikes on the Inca trail, ancient ruins, lush jungles, bustling cities and tropical beaches were just some of the places I explored as I guided people from around the world into what felt like the cusp of the unknown. My intention at the time was to work in this region and experience the Andes and the Amazon for one year before I would find a 'real' job for my career. It was a few months after my Master's graduation, and the opportunity appeared unexpectedly. I was in a group interview for environmental education programs in South America when a travel representative entered and announced a search for tour leaders in Peru. Being a group of Spanish-speaking educators, we were prime candidates for this opportunity, and I spontaneously sent an application. When I learned that the job I applied for was actually a volunteer position, I was on a plane to Bolivia two months later.

The training started in La Paz, Bolivia for a twenty-one-day tour to Lima, Peru. It would traverse cities, salt flats, deserts, the Andes and include a hike on the Inca trail to Machu Picchu. On my arrival day, I landed a few city blocks from the hotel where I was to meet the trainer. It was the middle of the afternoon and I had my backpack and paper in my hand with the directions as I made my way to the hotel. I was very cautious as I weaved through the bustling street vendors on a typical weekday when suddenly, something wet from above landed on me and dripped down my backpack, shoulders, and even on my head. Immediately, a man appeared in front of me with a kind, apologetic smile, asking if I was okay and handing me a white, clean, and what appeared to be a brand new handkerchief. Looking at him in a slight state of panic, I smiled to appreciate the kind gesture, and right away, I knew something was wrong. I felt a very clear sense of danger in the crowded city street, and I had to get away as quickly as possible. Refusing his handkerchief, I thanked him and quickly walked the next block to the arrival hotel. I found a washroom and wiped my face, hair, and backpack and prepared to meet the guide in the next few minutes. I was just on time.

When I met the guide, I greeted him with a big, warm "hello," not mentioning the incident. I was new to South America, adventure travel, my new leadership role and, I wanted to step into it gracefully. We exchanged pleasantries, and after I got settled in the hotel, we later laughed about that initial meeting. He knew something was wrong because why would my hair and backpack be wet if I was just coming from the airport? I believe my intuitive senses saved me that day. In some countries, distractions are often thrown at tourists to divert their attention for the intention of a robbery that I had not been aware of at the time and never encountered again. I was grateful for my inner voice that warned me, and I felt I had passed an initiation on the first day in South America. Time would tell if I was ready for the multitude of encounters that would be ahead.

The lifestyle of leading adventure tours across countries in South America was full of excitement. I learned the art of balancing the role of leadership and self-care with ever-changing itineraries. The days could be tiring yet comfortable with charming hotels, delicious restaurants, and seeing beautiful places with people from around the world, each with their own unique stories. I found myself in central and remote regions engaging with all aspects of society and various cultures armed with only the knowledge, insight, and grace I had available. I greeted each opportunity with enthusiasm. In the first year, I worked in Bolivia and Peru and was then sent to the Mayan Riviera in Mexico, where I was thrilled to be in the sunny landscapes and beaches of Cancun. By this point, travel had become second nature to me. After half a year of being on the road, I learned that life was fast-paced and experiences were transient as each new adventure led to the next. More was about to unfold for me during these learning experiences when I led my first tour from Mexico to Guatemala.

I guess nothing says more about adventure travel than experiencing one of the most threatening events possible on a travel journey. It was around Christmas time, and I had a group of twelve people on a Mayan exploration of tacos, beaches, and ancient ruins. The tour took us across the Mexico and Guatemala border on our way to Antigua, and it was a long travel day that was usually uneventful. After the border crossing, while driving along a stretch of highway, two pick-up trucks filled with men waving guns out their windows pulled up beside us and shockingly began to force us off the road. Our driver immediately had to pull over and stop the vehicle as the men proceeded to get on board. They took over the driver's seat and turned around to drive back on the highway onto a road leading into a forest. Meanwhile, a man sat beside me in the front seat holding a gun, further indicating that our tour was no longer going in the direction we thought. When you are under this type of pressure, like what you think is life and death pressure, you don't really have time to think and, ironically, a lot of things go through your mind at the same time. For me, my emotional senses became extremely heightened towards the six or seven men who had taken over the vehicle and began speaking to the passengers in Spanish, and I had no choice but to listen.

There are certain things in life you can't plan for. In this case, even with a man holding a gun beside me, I could not have imagined that at that particular moment I would bring my attention to the group and begin to translate for the robbers. In fact, I felt ridiculous during the incident and in retrospect, I wonder what psychological trait I employed to operate so effectively under such pressure. I knew I was the only one who could understand what they were saying and I wanted to calm the extreme panic felt by the twelve passengers whose tour bus suddenly shifted into a real life scary movie. During this intense and dangerous situation, my senses remained on high alert, to say the least, and interestingly, the man next to me gave me immediate insight that he was not threatening. I know it sounds strange, but I felt the man beside me let me know, through his gentle movements and non-aggressive position of the gun, that we were going to be okay. On the other hand, there were several characters in that entourage that I would not give similar credit. If a few of these overtly harmful men had taken charge, this story could have had a more catastrophic experience and ending.

During the next hour or so, while the men continued to rob our possessions in the forest of Guatemala, we all experienced trauma that day. Our sense of safety in the world was threatened and the protected façade of society and laws were not held accountable. The men drove off and left us the keys and our recovering driver to take us to our next destination a few hours away where we filed police reports and took deep breaths of relief in the present moment. I immediately returned to Canada for rest and recuperation and was given the option to consider completing the remainder of my first-year contract. I decided I wanted to put my feet back on the ground and continue. I thought it best to overcome possible trauma that could potentially be imprinted on me and have some unknown future consequences. I returned to Peru and was well received in the Andes with open arms.

During the next eight years or so, I worked as a freelance guide throughout most of South America while exploring other opportunities. I dabbled in several global paths such as environmental education, environmental consulting, herbal medicine making and becoming a certified yoga teacher connecting to healing that continued to be an important part of my foundation. I continued to feel a strong call to guide in South America, where my senses were continually opened to incredible experiences, including a season being on an expedition ship in Antarctica. The cruises would take us to the remote edges of the planet with waves of endless ocean, sounds of silence and gazing at crystalline glaciers to witness colonies of seals and penguins staring back at us. It was magical. The South American continent and beyond was an inspiration for me, and I eventually based myself in Rio de Janeiro, where I combined my experience of wellness and travel to create a travel agency for yoga retreats in Brazil and Peru.

Shifting my perspective from adventure traveler to entrepreneur required new skills and perceptions that I was uncertain I had but determined to embrace. It took great focus and effort to fulfill my vision, and after a few years, as the wellness travel agency grew, I thought I was growing with it. Living in Rio de Janeiro, Brazil also brought out the '*jeito*' or way of doing things with a 'hustler' mindset that I found exciting, yet put great pressure on me despite the fact I was offering wellness retreats. It was a learning process, and as a recovering people pleaser, I realized I had created a life where I measured my value on external production rather than my own self-worth.

The shift into this awareness and embodying my truth began with quantum healing. The quantum field is the place where all healing takes place and peels off our layers. I learned how to access tools and operate from a solid emotional and mental foundation that could support my life, my business and accept all parts of me in the process. By this time, I had returned to Canada and was living in Vancouver and spending extended periods of time at a friend's cabin on Vancouver Island. The balance between the city and escape to the serenity and isolation of the forest calmed me and offered time and space for deep reflection. Having to live my truth and be authentic meant I had to face my pain, be vulnerable and release the shame of my traumatic past to feel worthy.

In quantum healing, we access our Higher Self and connect with the consciousness of the original divine blueprint of our soul. We explore our inner foundations to embody our unique wholeness. We become witnesses to our memories and timelines and listen to the stories we tell ourselves with compassion. The shift into quantum healing has taken me from leading a life of adventure to an inner journey accessing higher and multidimensional realms. It has also taken me from guiding people in travel and yoga adventures to exploring journeys of consciousness for deep connection and inner transformation. It has been a profound shift for me. These days, when I listen to the voices around me, whether it is in a forest, city, or mountains, I feel a connection across time, space and dimensions and I am grateful for the experiences that have defined and liberated me into the grace of my divine calling.

About the Author

TARA CAMPBELL

Tara Campbell has always been an educator, leader, and a healer of various kinds. She began with the practice of yoga at a young age and has spent decades immersed in spiritual, travel, and nature exploration. Tara completed a degree in Anthropology with fieldwork in India and a Masters in Environmental Studies. Her research in Costa Rica focused on sensory connections to nature and medicinal plant healing. Tara has also trained with a herbalist, making traditional herbal medicine and developing environmental education programs.

Tara fell into the world of adventure travel in Latin America, where she explored countries for almost a decade, eventually inspiring her to connect wellness with travel. She developed a travel agency, leading yoga retreats in Brazil and Peru.

Tara was drawn to quantum healing after discovering she had internal wounding and patterns that challenged her perspective and goals. Tara now integrates her adventurous spirit, healing connections and intuitive consciousness to guide others on transformational journeys.

website: www.awakenedintegration.ca

Facebook: www.facebook.com/awakenedintegration

Instagram: www.instagram.com/awakenedintegration

CHAPTER 9
Forging Rebirth
MAGGIE MOORE

Y ou learn everything about yourself when you lose everything.

Five words and six seconds were all it took.

We were "that" couple... the ones that still held hands after seventeen years of marriage, the ones that looked forward to the end of our days together. I adored John, and he adored me right back. Our son, Collin, would count on his best friend, his father, to know exactly what to say all the time. When Collin was happy, John knew what would put him over the moon. When Collin was sad, John knew exactly what to say to cheer him up. It was a relationship I looked at with pride and no small amount of awe at its magic.

The day started just like any other for us. We were at the hospital neurology department for a routine medical appointment to test my son's ADHD to see how effective his current medications were in helping him focus. We both dropped him off, and I stayed to take him home. Because my son had gone right into the testing, they did not want to interrupt it, so John settled for the hug and "I love you," he said to Collin, and headed off to start his workday after giving me the hug, kiss, and an "I love you." I remember feeling so very blessed to be in this place, that I had a strong marriage despite the storms that life had been tossing at us lately.

After the testing was finished, I took Collin for breakfast, dropped him off at school, and went about my workday. I knew my husband was going directly from work to help some friends at a community organization. He spoke to me in the car on the way. He was heading into a bad cell zone and told me he loved me before the call dropped. Dropped calls happened every day when he passed that location.

Five words. Six seconds.

So, I went about my evening. Collin and I had dinner and were watching a little TV when he looked out the window and said, "Mom, there's a police car in the driveway." We have a good relationship with the police, so I really thought nothing of it, other than laughing to myself that there was likely a lost cat, a community situation, or maybe someone was up to some mild mischief in the neighborhood and he was there to ask if we'd seen anything.

Not wanting to get Collin distracted from our attempts to buckle down and do some homework, I sent my son to his room anyway and went to the door to answer the doorbell, expecting to help in any way I could and get my son started on his homework.

The police officer asked to come in, and there was a woman behind him. I let him in, and he started asking me a series of questions.

"Are you John Moore's wife?"

"Yes."

"Have you spoken to your husband this evening?"

"Yes" (At the time, I was thinking in my head, "I bet he did something silly like locking the keys in the car... I am sure going to tease him about this one.")

The woman behind him introduced herself as the Assistant Coroner.

Five words.

"There's been a terrible accident."

Six seconds was all it took to register the words and set the fuse alight.

My world exploded like a neutron bomb.

I heard a "snap" in my head that blasted through my body.

I felt the bottom falling out of our world, disappearing beneath our feet at breakneck speed like a landslide.

A shroud of sand seemed to bury me, making it difficult to breathe, difficult to think, and difficult to process what was being said. Everything shattered, burying me in the icy frost of unimaginable, unfathomable grief.

I thought that was the worst moment of my life.

It wasn't.

Thirty minutes later, that came.

Surrounded by friends who I told in a haze of pain sitting next to me, I had the most impossible task of my life: telling my son his father was never coming home.

And I blew it.

I reached for a pitiful, useless platitude that I had heard at funerals over the years. I told my son that God needed another angel and that he had called Daddy home.

"God doesn't need daddy. We do. Here. Now. I.WANT.MY.DADDY" screamed my son, grief and shock etched into his baby face. He howled with his entire body and soul, then an animalistic cry of grief and pain that seared itself into my soul and haunted my nightmares for years.

I made the calls that night robotically to my in-laws, with my frozen heart shattering even more when I had to tell my mother-in-law her son would never be seen again. Then to my family who had swept up John and locked him to their hearts as surely as he was locked to mine. My sister Rose, absorbing the shock, did not skip a beat and told me she would be on a plane from out of state as soon as she could.

This is the way we deal with an unexpected death in America-we put the person who is the least able to decide in the position of making the hardest ones.

Somehow, I finished the calls. My dear friends Angie and Todd offered to stay. I declined. I promised to take something to make me sleep. I lied. The first of many grieving widows lies. I would not leave my son with nightmares he could not name without being there before he finished his first sob. Fortunately, he cried so hard he fell asleep.

And they left me sitting on the steps, staring at the front door. The door that now seemed like the door to our bank vault had slammed shut on our old life with a resounding clang... and then someone destroyed the key. The door that, on some level, I knew my husband would never come through again, but while I knew the thought, it seemed to slip away and I couldn't grasp it, like a sound you hear vaguely through a series of doors. Muffled. Barely understandable. Shock, blessed shock, had wrapped me in the deep safety of her covers so I could contemplate the cataclysm of his death, be it ever so slightly.

I got to bed. I tossed and turned and couldn't sleep until I buried my head in the scent of my husband on his pillow and I think I slept. Maybe? Dreams I couldn't remember haunted me.

I remember waking up early, and the events of the previous evening barely penetrated my shock-numbed brain, like a sharp knife slicing cleanly through its target but not disturbing any other part of the meal. My shock was deepening, but my reasoning was somewhat intact.

As I sat in the chair, I dealt with crises the way I had learned to do from an early age... ruthlessly assassinating the problem until it was dead or nearly dead and could not threaten me or those I loved, and in the quiet of the solution afterward, let loose the emotion I had bottled up while solving the problem. Set the fear aside, deal with the issue, and then, in victory, allow yourself to feel what you could not at the time. And it had worked, so I did it here, too.

I had a few challenges to deal with. I was in a terrible place to be a widow... Aren't we all?. I did not mention that I did not walk to the front door. I crutched. On our last vacation (though I did not know it at the time), a few months prior, I had fallen and torn my knee. Two surgeries later (the most recent for an infection), I was back at the beginning of physical therapy and strengthening my knee to walk again. My crutches were sitting at my side.

As I sat in the chair, I stared dully at the piles and boxes piled in our living room. We had had a flood in our basement, and our basement was torn down to the studs in the wall for my husband to refinish. All of our rescued items from downstairs were stacked haphazardly around me. And because of my weight restrictions, I could lift nothing bigger or heavier than a loaf of bread. Besides our corporate jobs, we had purchased a laundromat as a turnaround business prior to our vacation. My family and in-laws both lived 1,000 miles away in another state.

And in my job, I had the company's annual salary bonus plan going into the payroll systems in less than ten days.

I remember sitting there in the chair, crutches at my side, leg aching, looking dully around the room and realizing that there was no way in hell I could possibly do this on my own, and for the first time in my life, I could not see a way to get it done. My husband had been dead for less than twelve hours. I had no clue what to do next.

And yet, I had no choice.

Because there was a little boy sleeping in the next room who meant everything to me, and a stepdaughter five states away. They were my husband's legacy in this world.

I faced a very ugly and cruel truth that every widowed person, especially those of us who are parents, faces as the sunrise filtered through the window: I had to make this work, because If I went back to bed and crawled into the grave with my husband when we buried him, I was burying all of us alive.

For a few minutes, I gave in to the pain by crying from my soul at the loss. Sobs tore my chest like razor blades as I silently sobbed my grief and terror to the universe.

And then, I stopped.

I decided… to take the next right step.

I resolved to take one step, then another, and I was going to figure this out, to "triumph" over this challenge simply because I had no choice.

Boy, was I a fool.

I slammed into widowhood like a diver doing a belly flop off a high diving board. Grief sucks up every bit of breath you have and then some. It detonates the life you had like an EF5 twister, leveling the life you knew-and your entire self along with it.

RIP to the life you had.

Because you have to dismantle absolutely everything you built in your life together-joint accounts, retitle assets, untangle absolutely everything you were joined at the hip on. Decide guardians. Beneficiaries. Lose your name. Your identity as a wife. As a couple. As a parent.

And you're doing it all, making decisions, guiding children at times, in a world where every breath, every move is an effort, like you are encased in refrigerated molasses and must push through.

Grief levels you. It levels your life. It is a thief of dreams because it strips you of the life you planned, together in the faraway someday. The first time I had to fill out a form that gave two options, "married" or "single," I used my pen like a sword, carving "widowed" in there and checking the home-drawn box with righteous rage.

Grief is a forge. It burns away the life you knew.

But in that wreckage, you transform. Once you accept that you have no choice but to change, possibilities appear. You're on that voyage, even if you were shanghaied onto the ship by your spouse's death. You're going anyway on the cruise from hell where death is the travel agent with grief as the cruise director. Anchors away! They just burned the dock behind you. No going back to the life you knew.

The grief is so brutal and so all-consuming that it burns away the life you knew. It takes you down to your core and the basis of your existence. The neurological trauma is so deep that you can walk into a room five, six, or seven times and forget why you were there. I lost track of days, weeks even. Time stretched interminably and disappeared with the flick of a wrist.

Everything I had hoped for, dreamed for, built for, and planned for was shattered like the glass in the windshield of a crumpled car. Reassembling that life of shattered shards is just as impossible as that windshield. There will always be cracks and a chasm where my best friend should be.

My life was not the one I chose, but it was now a blank slate. A few anchors remained: my children, my job, my in-laws, my friends, and my family.

You can't think in grief, but you can function. You build up from the animal basics: food, clothing, shelter, and work. Kids first, then you, somewhere in the background. Your life becomes a god-awful mess that you hide from the outside world. I earned an Oscar every single week.

Slowly, I learned ways to make this journey easier. I learned that grief is like a bottle of soda. Every wave is a shake and if you keep the cap on, it will explode when you can't afford it to, all over the work meeting you HAVE to be present for, the school meeting you are desperately trying to keep together, and the year of the firsts (first holiday, first birthday, first Mother's or Father's Day). But if you figure out a way to put together opportunities for a controlled release, a slow "hiss" to let the pressure off, you can prevent or minimize those moments.

I learned that people will insert themselves into your journey, provide unsolicited advice and commentary on your life, and judge how "well" you are grieving, as if this is some kind of journey to the grief Olympics and you are training for that Gold Medal by how much effort you put forth to appear normal. I learned to hate those comments as much as I hungered for them, at least someone saw I was still alive, even if I felt dead inside. Inside, you realize very quickly that throwing more "effort" at grief doesn't work. This isn't a training ground, it's a transformation ground. Your old life has been torn away and replaced with a trauma that you need to lead your family through.

I learned deep gratitude for the people at my workplace, who showed up for me in so many ways, just as I had shown up for them. I was deeply grateful to the people who listened to me when I stopped their platitudes with, "Please… no one knows what to say to us… and we don't know what to say back either." And the masks would drop, and they could be real with me again, instead of parroting phrases that hurt like rubbing alcohol on a cut.

I learned appreciation and kindness for the people who helped me as they were able, within the limitations of their heart and soul, like the neighbor who came over and said, "I suck at the grief stuff-but I can clean your kitchen" and proceeded to do just that.

I learned that grief is not just the detonation of your life in a neutron bomb, but also a very real, ongoing trauma to your heart and mind. I learned that the memory issues that accompany widowhood are normal. I learned to function with a brain that was like a sieve. I also learned that grief functions differently in ADHD brains. I watched my son spending time after school make up for two years of lost learning in one year. He did this from his grief zombie response so he could be college-ready.

I learned what in my life was not essential, and the forced drought of energy made me discard it all. I learned to appreciate the simplicity of happiness when it came the first time, like a child opening that first present on Christmas morning. I clutched at that happiness like the gift it was, hoping it would not pop like a fragile soap bubble and disappear into the deep, drowning, water of my grief.

And then, the phone call came. Tentative, and cautious, to my work line.

"Maggie, I know you miss John. We miss him too. I can't imagine what you're going through, but my best friend's husband died suddenly-can you help?"

I did.

And another…

"Maggie, you're handling this so well. Can you help me? I just took this top HR role, and one of our execs lost his wife to a heart attack. We're doing this huge acquisition. How can we help and support him?"

I did.

And another.

I realized there are so many myths out there about grief that lead to needless suffering. I read journals and learned about the basis of trauma and how it affects us. I learned that so much needs to change, and I keep learning every day.

While I was healing others, I healed myself.

And in the process, I learned to return to myself, my true self, before the world wrapped me in expectations and veneers that hid the power of an authentic life. All the things I'd learned and studied about grief, I taught to others. I became a student of my loss and the grieving transformation. By going from desolation to transformation, I was able to lead others on that path.

The forge of grief changed me into something different, and yet the same. I came home to myself when I had to put the pieces back together and curate a new life out of the shards of the old one.

No one asks to be widowed.

But in being widowed, I found my calling for the next season of my life.

It was how I became The Widow Coach... and began bringing hope to others.

About the Author
MAGGIE MOORE

Widowhood is a moment of rebirth, to integrate your spouse's legacy while you create a life you love.

In The Voyage and the Return, Maggie explodes myths about widowhood in her story that is an intimate snapshot of crippling tragedy and a clarion call of hope. She says "A spouse's death shatters your life into pieces like a dropped vase. You can't reconstruct the life you had….but it is a chance to build a new mosaic from the pieces of the old life and create something new and vibrant."

The death of her husband John suddenly in an auto accident in 2014 detonated the life she knew, catapulting her into an alternate universe of widowhood- one that no one prepares you for. You learn who you are when you lose who you were. It's a moment to evolve and become a truer version of yourself.

As a Speaker, Author, Widow Coach & Certified Grief Recovery Specialist®, Maggie Moore uses practical tools of her Widowed Navigator® and Widowed Compass® training to manage the widowed process, enabling transformational coaching from the inside out.

She's been featured as an expert guest on podcasts like *Widowed But Not Alone*. As a sought-after speaker for business service, church and community conferences, she warmly educates about how to help the grieving. Maggie provides professional development education to estate attorneys, business and HR leaders, financial planners, wealth managers, business and professional associations in meetings or as a conference speaker.

She loves life and can be found on adventures with friends and family: hiking, blowing glass, kayaking, ziplining with her son in unusual places, badly attempting to learn Chinese brush painting, or finding another National Park to explore.

Book a free consultation with Maggie at: www.calendly.com/thewidowcoach

Get practical advice on widowhood, download free ebooks, sign up for my newsletter and free gift, hear podcast interviews and see topics I speak about at The Widow Coach | Resources www.linktr.ee/thewidowcoach

Like and follow my Facebook page at: www.facebook.com/thewidowcoach

SCAN ME

Scan to claim your 15+ page BONUS guide.

CHAPTER 10

THE DARKEST NIGHTS

MOIRA CAMINO

My journey of self-discovery began when I was 21 years old. Because of some extreme difficulties, I was forced to abandon my university course during the final year and then left home. I moved into a shared house with my then-boyfriend and his friends. This meant that I left all my old comforts behind, such as a guaranteed roof over my head, food on the table, and enough money for bills and rent. I now had to learn how to make my way in the real world.

This was a bit of a shock to the system but also an exhilarating time as it was the new start I'd been craving for so long, to live my life without judgement or criticism as an independent person who didn't have to answer to anyone. I just had to learn to provide everything for myself, including my mental and emotional health.

A little while in, I started to feel completely disconnected and somehow knew that I needed to go through a spiritual change or upgrade of some sort or else I would inevitably spiral through a very difficult time, but I worried that this was going to rock the boat and perhaps create a difficult situation for myself. Not listening to my intuition and not having a spiritual mentor during that time caused me to go through a couple of years of the darkest night of the soul, whereby I felt completely disconnected from the richness of life and my happiness. I could only mainly see the darkness in others and in the world around me, which was a very frightening and dark place to be. I felt a complete shutdown of all things good and many unresolved issues and traumas from a (short-ish) lifetime of feeling like the odd one out, being a sensitive empath who took on the issues of others, not feeling seen or heard, as well as intense feelings of not being good enough, surfaced. Of course, during that time I didn't have the ability to pinpoint all of the issues that were shouting to be heard and identify where they stemmed from, as I was not in touch with all of my emotions and I didn't have the tool kit or maturity to work on them all yet. I would later come to realize that my soul was calling me to take action.

REMEMBERING...

A good friend at the time booked me and a few others onto a spiritual retreat, whereby I met a speaker who spoke of this darkest night. I was delighted to hear what she had to say and fully resonated with it all. At last, I knew what my affliction was; my soul was calling to me!

On that same day, I met a wonderful lady called Lettie, who had a stand there with some crystals. She gestured for me to pick one up and as I held it I felt an immense connection with this crystal being, and from that moment, something that had lain dormant inside me came to life. I had now found my purpose, working with crystals! This started my love of all things crystals and a lifetime of working with them and helping others to find out who they really are and learn to love and accept themselves for all that they are.

From that point forward, and over the years, I learned more and more about working with energy, crystals, channeling, and healing. I started awakening to and learning more about who I am and why I incarnated on this earth over and over again throughout the centuries. Each time learning more while refining my skills and connecting more deeply to my sovereignty. Most of all, I felt the pure connection of love between myself and others and knew that my gift was to help others discover their skills and gifts and more fully come into their own power.

I also remembered, through my own self-healing process and with the support from some wonderful mentors and healers, that I'm entitled to have respect, joy, and pure love in my life. That I have the power to heal all past issues and trauma, not just mine but also from my long ancestral lines. At the beginning of our healing journey, we can feel like we're working in the dark and fumbling around blindly. However, once we start delving into our issues and blocks, we are able to identify the root cause and can start to see the family patterning, issues, and trauma. We can go into past lives and heal them, clear and integrate them, and bring all of that beautiful photonic energy of healing back into our physical body. Also bringing the soul fragments that had been released out of the body through traumatic experiences back in and becoming more fully embodied. Realising that you're your own sovereign being and truest self, that you don't have to answer to anyone or anything other than yourself, and that you know your divine purpose and connect with your heart and soul.

HEALING...

I now help others to connect to their sovereign/soul self and their own gold print of living light intelligence, which then comes flooding into their body as beautiful and harmonic light frequencies. I also help to bring in their soul templates, all that they are, which then creates a shift within all of the cells in their body and brain, creating new, much healthier neural pathways. When working one-to-one, I create meditations specific for that person that they can do for 3 to 6 weeks to fully embody that healing permanently so that they can then access more of their wonderful gifts: self-forgiveness, self-compassion, and most importantly, self-love. Their love for themselves and others then increases and connects them to unity consciousness, therefore, enabling them to come more fully into 5D consciousness with more ease. They can then become a full expression of themselves as they are through love and light, and they can then access their innate gifts and power without having to look to others to help them get their power.

I never imagined that I would be able to help my clients release past life blocks and fears that had previously made it impossible for them to feel fulfilled during this lifetime. Witnessing many of them stepping into their power and becoming the successful healers that they have dreamt of being is why I do this work.

About the Author

MOIRA CAMINO

Moira Camino is an intuitive healer and an empath who works with multi-dimensional and liquid crystal frequencies from Andromeda, Atlantis, and Lemuria. She combines these with the cosmic medicine wheel, Celestial beings, Masters and freestyle channelling to give a thorough and unique healing modality.

Moira works to bring alignment between the person and their higher and sovereign self, whilst balancing their masculine and feminine energies and clearing past life trauma that is currently affecting them.

She mainly works with other healers or those already on their spiritual path. The healing she offers can be seen as a fast track for those who wish to embody more fully who they truly are and to enable them to move forward in life, especially from a stuck place or situation.

Moira also teaches others how to activate their light body (Merkaba) so that they can become more 5th-dimensional in their 3rd-dimensional bodies. She does Akashic Records Readings, which have helped many to get clear on their purpose and find ways to make their dreams come true.

Connect with Moira: www.wonderfulyouhealing.com

Tune in to listen to here Smoky-Quartz Guided Meditation:

https://www.wonderfulyouhealing.com/smoky-quartz-guided-meditation/

CHAPTER 11
A Rose Blooms When You're Ready

JENNIFER FAI ARMITAGE

Four years into solo parenthood and career, I started dreaming. Dreaming of a life full of goodness, joy, and abundance. Usually, this dream would come after a phone call at work from my kid's daycare.

"Hey Jen, you're going to have to pick up your boy. He hurt another kid, and his parents won't leave till they see and talk to you." This was a weekly occurrence. I wish I was exaggerating, but I'm not. We went through seven daycares and on top of that, parents wanted to have it out with me at each one.... There was no help, and I felt hopeless. Doctors told me it's just a phase but we will send you to some specialists for a more in-depth look at his behavior. Years and years on waitlists... I would think to myself, "What am I doing wrong, I just want my son to be happy and succeed in life. Why don't I know how to support him?"

When kindergarten started, I felt relieved. The teachers and school will have all the resources and help for us. We're saved! Little did I know, it was another dead end for me and my son. Still waiting for doctors' appointments, the calls from the daycares turned into calls from the school—suspensions and endless meetings. I remember arriving at the meetings, peeling myself out of the car, and trying to control my heart palpitations so I could walk to and speak during the meetings. I felt completely alone and lost. My stress and anxiety were unbearable and came out in spontaneous crying fits at work and nervous breakdowns in the car or grocery store. Not to mention the metaphorical 'cracks' that kids fall through in the school system. I didn't quite understand what this metaphor meant, but I do now, and we found them.

I knew what I wanted and needed. That is to be with my kids all the time, but I needed to work full time. How do I do this? I need this, they need this. How do I do this? I would always come back to this thought randomly while driving, in the shower, or during work… "What's the secret to joy, love, and abundance in career, parenthood, and life—together?" I know there's an answer. There has to be more to my life and my family's life than this.

Years continue to go by, still juggling, stressing, and wondering "what's the secret?" and "I need to find it!" One night, after tucking my kids into bed, after they had a bad day at school with bullies who followed them home, resulting in a call to the police. I was telling them how amazing they are and how lucky I am to be their mother. I went to my room, closed the door, and cried harder than I had ever cried before. I'm not a religious person; I didn't know how to pray or meditate, but I asked and begged… out loud… "PLEASE HELP ME, help me, please. I don't know what I'm doing; I love my kids more than life, and they deserve love and kindness from this world! So do I! Please help me find it!"

As I'm on my knees, sobbing, my son comes in and asks, "Mom, what's wrong? Why are You crying on the floor?"

I got up and said, "I just stubbed my toe, honey bunny. Thank you for checking on me! Now you get back to bed, d'ar boy! Love you, sweet dreams!" And off he went. At this point, I was ready for my relaxing hot shower, a few deep breaths, and then sleeeep.

The next day, I took my kids to school, dropped them off at their classrooms, and headed to the office. I had a meeting with the principals regarding the bullying my kids are facing. They both come in, say their pieces, and send me on my way. On my way out, I noticed two boys coming in from outside. As I pass them, I hear this behind me, this bellowing yell from a teacher, "TAKE OFF YOUR TOQUE! NO HATS IN THE SCHOOL OR DETENTION AND THE TOQUES GONE!"

I shot my head around and asked the teacher, "over wearing a toque?" If this was your tolerance and anger towards the bullying that happens here, we wouldn't have this problem. Your standards or code of conduct are so broken. I left mad, angry, heartbroken, and sad.

Years continue to go by, still juggling, stressing, and wondering when am I going to find the secret to a blissful life and start living it! But nothing happened... no changes, except summer break. But YAY! No more school to deal with, just work for me! And off to work I go! Dropping my kids off at my parent's house and getting to work, unaware that today would be the day that changed my life forever... the blessing I've been asking for happened! Of course, though, at the time I didn't know that it was a blessing. While I was completing a task, done every day, all day for the past ten years, I managed to lacerate the tendons in my wrist and median nerve while opening a box with an Exacto knife. In my defense, it was a spanking brand new knife, right out of the box! But still, I cut my arm really badly. Lost permanent feeling in my upper arm, wrist, and index. A career ending workplace accident.

I was DEVASTATED. I lost my work family, my best friends, and my career! This place was my bread and butter for my little family and home. All I thought was "now what do I do?" Try to heal as best I can and get back to it. But that wasn't the case. I didn't heal the way my doctor, the Workers' Compensation Board (WCB), or I had hoped. Seeing the specialist for the last time confirmed it. He told me an improvement to my injury wasn't likely and I would be left with the way it was. All of the horror stories I heard about dealing with the Workers' Compensation Board I found out were true. Cutting my payments off while recovering and desperately needing help with daily chores I couldn't do. This created a whole new area of stress and sleepless nights, on top of my son falling through the cracks and my kids receiving threats and harassment at school. But what really drove me crazy was not being able to do the dishes! I ended up disputing my stopped payments case with WCB and won. It took over a year, but I won.

So I decided to use my back pay, from WCB, for continued learning. I felt like a kid in a candy store! "What should I take?" I love history and exploring our beautiful land! I love love love traveling too! There's my career! I'm going to be a local Tour guide/operator! I went back to school and took Travel and Tourism. Ahhh I'm so happy and excited, I thought, "How many people actually get to work their dream job?! I don't know, but how lucky am I to be one of them!"

Once my moment began, I began building itineraries and networking with other operators from around the world! I felt unstoppable! Until I was stopped... dead in my tracks. All my hard work and hours away from my family started bubbling up deep inside me while listening to the news. We are in a pandemic and are shutting down the world till we have COVID contained. My heart stopped. Obviously, I was devastated that there was a pandemic, something you don't think would happen in your lifetime, but all my hard work and dreams were crushed. Though I am a positive person and have always looked at the glass as half full, I thought this is ok, just another life event and everyone's experiencing it. We'll get through it stronger. In the meantime, let's find something to do.

I really liked what the 'Centre of Excellence' offered, and even better, they're accredited! So I signed up for meditation, Reiki, and hypnotherapy. I started them casually - for there was no rush, there's no time limit to complete, and we're in a pandemic with no end in sight.

So many times while learning about and exploring my own meditation practice, I'd catch myself talking to myself or having moments of pure bliss and love or crying so hard my eyes would swell.

And Reiki! I was so proud when I received my master's diploma... My grandma was a Reiki Master and I remember her telling me stories of clients she'd help heal with cancers and how they beat it. Who wouldn't want to learn this? Even just as a hobby, I thought, what a great skill to have! I brought this into my daily routine for me and my kids.

I very much enjoyed the courses and continued to take more. I practiced on myself a lot and continued to practice hypnotherapy healing on my kids. Now, I'm feeling confident enough to practice with my friends and family. I started to combine all the courses I took into one practice and came up with 'Distance Healing Sessions' via Zoom. I'll never forget the session that changed my life forever. A lady from the US, referred by a friend, had just booked. I didn't know her or her story, but right away, I knew she was sick. At the start of the session, I kept hearing 'her liver.' As we went deeper and deeper, I said over and over, 'psoriasis of the liver?.' Then I kept being shown her liver, through her body. It was like how Google Maps zoom into your location from a satellite. I was also shown her liver trying to repair itself over and over again. I told the lady after and shared my notes. She was at a loss for words because the doctor had just talked to her about her liver counts two days before. A couple of weeks later, she told me she had psoriasis of the liver from years of heavy drinking. I was floored. I knew, then. This is what I'm meant to do.

I fell in love with this new practice. One day, after a session with a dear friend of mine, she asked if I had heard of Edgar Casey. He was an American clairvoyant who channeled while asleep in a trance-like state in the early 1900s.

I fell in love with his work, continued my learning with his teachings, and incorporated them into my distance healing sessions.

I felt so lucky to have found such a beautiful hobby!

Six months into the pandemic, I decided I wanted a side hustle. Tourism is still shut down, but salons are opening. I always loved making people feel good and feel beautiful. My mom and sister love getting their lashes done, but it's so expensive. If I learn this, then that's another thing they don't have to pay for! I started looking around for lash tech courses and found one online. I enrolled and couldn't wait to start! Though for me, realizing there are things you can learn online... and lash extensions was NOT one of them. I tried, I really did. But still failed. I said to heck with it. I tried my best, but it's not for me.

Tourism will come back soon. I kept telling myself. So I kept meditating, practicing energy healing, mindfulness, gratitude, and clairvoyance. I loved it. And actually... I started to notice the benefits of these practices in my everyday life. I started to gain confidence and speak up for myself. I was becoming more aware of my unswerving ego's self-talk and how I treated myself. I remember thinking "I'm glad I'm not married to me; I don't treat myself very nice." That's when I realized I needed to treat myself with more love and compassion. You'd think it'd be easy, but I've been bullying and nitpicking myself and everything I do for as long as I can remember. How do I stop doing this? I started by using my mindfulness and Reiki practices. Just for today, I will not worry, I will not be angry, I will be grateful, I will do my work honestly, I will be kind to every living thing and count my Blessings." Talk about reprogramming. I learned that the only way this mantra will work is if I am present, in the moment, and paying attention to every word and feeling I get when speaking these words. This statement came in very handy the following week when all my traveling guests were canceling their bookings and no longer postponing. I completely understood why, but it was still devastating. My local tour guide career was over.

I broke. My mental health was maxed, along with my kids' (all three of us developed social anxiety; it's real and debilitating), and all my hard work was gone. The days went on as I had the biggest pity party. While laying in bed, feeling sorry for myself, I had an epiphany. This thought came out of nowhere... 'This isn't the end. Right now would be a great time to learn how to deal with stress and anxiety. Something you've been trying to do for years!'

Therapists and counselors... making peace, forgiving, letting go, healing, loving again, blah blah blah... That's what they help you do, right? Of course.. and I tried it... I thought it was great! But it wasn't for me. I still needed more and to go deeper, but I wasn't willing. My problem was that I didn't open up fully. I couldn't. I wasn't comfortable. Every time I walked into the counselor's office, I felt nervous and anxious. I didn't want to be here. I don't want to open up, I don't want to relive old trauma that I had spent years burying. The reason why I came to counseling is to deal with stress/anxiety around my career and home. And this counselor is trying to dig deeper. I thought, 'This is not what I wanted; what she's asking of me is too much. Just show me how to deal with stress and sleepless nights, please! I'll be fine.' That's all I wanted... Not to uncover decades of mental and physical abuse from men I've spent years burying. I didn't even want to know them again. I didn't want her to know my past either, but the reality of it was that I didn't want to feel them again. Those memories and traumas are buried deep for a reason— though, they still bubbled up when triggered. Like when my kids' coaches would yell or scream, it brought me back to those old traumas, and it was so debilitating. My anxiety attacks were overwhelming, and I'd have to leave to do breathwork in my car. Deep down, I knew I had to dig them back up in order to heal — and be the Jennifer I knew I was and came here to be! So I said yes, ok, let's try a new counselor.

Just before the session started, I thought, "ok Jennifer, it's time to stop being timid, closed off, and letting life happen to you... YOU make life happen for you. Therapy is the answer. And it's time to heal, let go, and forgive. We'll go through all the uncomfortable things together. You want to be the best version of yourself, right? Just do the work here; it's safe. It's time to shine." I kept saying this over and over again to myself. But how am I going to get through this? I wasn't feeling this therapist. I tried another one, but I didn't like that one either. So I just stopped.

Still, in the same place, I decided to get a tarot reading from a friend, a psychic medium. She told me what I already knew. I need lots of inner work done and to work through ALL of it. At this point, I was well into my spiritual awakening, connecting on a quantum level and seeing how hypnosis and meditation go hand in hand. I asked her about past life regressions, they intrigued me so much. She didn't do them but suggested someone who could... Jennifer Dawn, my hero and mentor!

That's how my healing began. A past life regression. Her soothing and tranquil voice carried me through my childhood, adult, and past life memories. Bringing light to trauma/blocks and releasing them. In turn, leaving space for only goodness, love, and absolute bliss.

What is the secret to living a life full of bliss? You. You are the secret. Heal yourself. Know yourself. Make yourself whole and free. Release all limits, so your love can flow unconditionally, for yourself and all. This will bloom your rose of bliss in your heart completely. And it will guide you without fail.

By releasing trauma and healing, I discovered parts of me I didn't know existed. All my blocks of self-sabotage, doubt, and unworthiness gently left my whole being. After the healing, it's like finding lost treasures of talents, gifts, and wisdom from deep inside you. The more I regressed, healed, and healed others, the more I exposed and released what's holding me back. In turn, releasing the trauma and discovering how special I really am. The bonus was during my own healing and while healing others — My healing abilities grew immensely. Practicing Quantum Reiki with crystals developed my clairvoyance, claircognizance, and psychic touch. Psychic touch: I know where the blocks and pain lay. And when combined with energy medicine in massage, it goes even deeper and heals. And this is on a quantum level and not just for your body but also for your mind and soul.

As we work through physical knots, it releases and heals stuck, old emotional traumas and un-serving beliefs and paradigms stored in your physical cells and subconscious. It's hard to believe for some, but I am living proof that these spiritual practices are real and they heal! My life was completely transformed in the most beautiful ways using these practices, and I need to share this with the world.

As I practice more and more, my gifts become stronger. During meditation and each session with Jenn, I delved deeper and stronger into my mind, connecting with my higher self and my Guides. Just by simply asking for help and being open to receiving, the divine energies removed my past traumas and old paradigms. And we work as a team. That's another secret! 'Ask and you shall receive...' another old saying I know the meaning of now!

Science and religion KNOW there's unseen energy flowing through and binding us all together. A universal life force energy. Whatever you want to call it, god, prana, deity, it's the light inside all of us. We all practice universal co-creation (whether you know this or not) and we are all connected and made of the same energy, love — There is no stronger energy force. This I need to share with the world too.

I find that as our cosmology expands, our family, education, and political and religious institutions of modern human society spiral into decadents, narcissism, depravity, and nihilism. We can stop this because we operate on vibration. If we start healing ourselves, these healing vibrations will, in turn, heal the people around us, our planet, and the universe.

I realized the things I was trying to force were not for me. I AM. I know what that means now. My confidence skyrocketed as my inner strength grew infinitely! I love myself unconditionally, and when I think of this love I have for myself, it brings tears to my eyes. I look at EVERYTHING now mindfully, with compassion and pure love. No matter how lost or hopeless you feel, you are not alone, ever. You have a light inside of you, of divine pure love, and it is filled with tools and wisdom to live a blissful, abundant, full of love, and life! It's there for you when you're ready! Including Your soul and free will, those are yours and no one can take them from you. Always remember that.

About the Author

JENNIFER FAI ARMITAGE

"There has to be more to life... what's the secret to living a joyous, abundant, and full of life, LIFE?!"

Have you found yourself asking this? Jennifer Armitage did... A lot! That question was constantly on her mind.

After a career-ending workplace accident, she decided to follow her heart, and release past traumas and beliefs holding her back from her dreams of freedom. Freedom from the nine to five, freedom from living a life for others, and living up to other people's expectations. Living her life on her own terms with no bounds or limitations and the ultimate freedom to be 100% authentic and true to herself, her passion, and calling.

During the pandemic, she decided to focus on what made her light up. She started exploring her Spiritually and taking courses for fun during the pandemic. In turn, without realizing it, she started healing herself.

It's YOU. YOU are the secret! Jen knows it. YOU are the key to unlocking your soul-aligned, wildest dreams, love for life, and LIFE!

She's the Inventor of the Cyprys Wand, an object that removes natural and artificial sulphites, kills bacteria, viruses, and algae in liquids. The CEO of 'Rose of Bliss' Healing mind, body, and soul. She's a medium, intuitive Healer (in person and online), Psychic Touch masseuse, and sugar hair removal specialist. Most importantly she is a single parent of two beautiful kids, Mataya and Marcus.

Jennifer believes every one of us is here for a purpose and a mission. To accomplish, grow, co-create and live our most blissful soul-aligned lives, harmoniously! Jennifer knows now when you follow your inner compass and gut feelings fill yourself up with love and gratitude, you bloom into the most beautiful form of your true self. Her passion is to help women and men find their life of bliss and watch their beautiful bloom unfold.

Learn more and connect with Jennifer:

- **Cyprys Wand**: www.ishowonline.com
- **Rose of Bliss Facebook Group:** www.facebook.com/groups/1508224409579506/?ref=share
- **Jennifer's Facebook Page:** www.facebook.com/groups/1508224409579506/user/100007985238480

CHAPTER 12
"They said, No"
STEPHANIE OLIVO

"The investors are going to hold off right now." – was one of the last conversations I had with Dirk that day. Dirk was my husband of 5 years, and we had recently decided to make me the majority owner to aid us in some medical contracts, but our business was on the decline. We had friends who connected us with Equity investors, and that day, July 20, 2017, was my call to see if they'd take us on to help us get liquid again.

Dirk was on edge. He had been on edge for a while. His son, my stepson, Kai, overdosed on heroin 14 months prior. This was turbulent for us personally and for our business - so everyone, quite frankly, was on edge.

"We can find someone else or sell the company to the team in Germany!" I said. I was simply over it. I was always taught that if you fail, you just cut your losses and move forward. He was taught a different way of doing things, and failure or quitting was not an option. He kept pushing different scenarios at me, and I was over it. I didn't want to hear it anymore, and I said, "It is what it is, and we have to find another plan." Looking back at that interaction, I don't think I had ever seen him so pale. The look on his face was of someone who had been defeated; this face I had never seen before in the 11 years together. He was silent. He turned around and left my office.

He returned and said, "I have to take some paperwork to Bob, and I'll be back later this afternoon." I was sitting at my desk, trying to figure out how we could manage the debt we had with the company and how much actual liquid we needed to release a shipment to sell, and I just looked up at him and said, "yeah, ok! Later." He kind of stood there for a second, and I wasn't sure if he wanted to say something else, but I think maybe that was the point where he wanted to say his final "goodbye" to me, but I don't think he physically could.

Dirk had been struggling for the last year with the death of Kai, and it was something that was affecting everything in our lives. There were times when he wouldn't come to work, wouldn't shower for days, and towards the end, he kept on mentioning killing himself. I would tell him, "Let's go to therapy," let's try this — let's try that, and he would, and it would be ok for a bit — but it was never enough. I don't know and may never know what it is to lose a child. I know unconditional love and would "give my life" for my niece and nephew, but the love of your own child—this I do not know. That pain, the sorrow, the hopelessness of what *I could have... I should have... I would have.*

It was about 12:30 when I tried to call Dirk, and he didn't pick up. At that time, we all had Instant Messenger on the computers because we'd always be on the phone and it was the easiest way to communicate with the staff. So I messaged him, "Hey, you coming back to the office?"

He replied, "Yeah, should be there around 3:30 pm."

I said "ok" and went on about my day. Around 3:30 pm, I messaged him again, "Hey, if you're not coming back in, that's ok — just need to know. We may have some other options for the company, and we can just talk to you at home."

No response.

4:00 pm: "You coming back or not?"

No response.

I wasn't worried this time, but I was annoyed. I didn't want to be at work either, so I decided to leave. I told the team and left. As I drove home, I was calling one phone after the other to let him know I was not at the office.

Voicemail.

When I arrived home, the SUV wasn't there. I was like, "ok — guess he's with Bob like he mentioned he'd be." I had the three dogs with me, so I dropped them off out back and decided to vacuum his car. As I finished up, I called the phone again. Nothing! I'm like, "This is so weird, he usually answers one of them." I'm calling and calling like a maniac.

As I'm walking up the stairs to shower, I call one of the phones again... I'm about halfway up the stairs when it rings, in the office downstairs. I turn around and walk down towards the office and notice that the computer is on, and there's a notepad with his scribble on it. Not paying attention, I try the other phone because I'm thinking, "ok, this phone is here, he must have the other." As the phone is ringing, I look down and focus on the scribble, and it is a note... from Dirk.

"Sorry, I'm such a failure. I should have hugged you before I left."

I sat down at the desk and thought to myself, "What is this? Is this what I think it is? Is he just writing this to tell me he's sorry for not hugging me before he left the office?" My mind wasn't racing because I believe I was in shock at what I was seeing in front of me. The computer was on a German page and I had no clue what was on the screen. I said, "ok, let me call Bob and see what's up."

"Bob, are you with Dirk?" I asked him. "No, he called me and I had to go to Sarasota and I couldn't meet him. Why? What's going on? Everything ok?", he asks. "Well, I am not sure now because he told me earlier he'd be with you, and I've been calling his phones and one is here and he's not answering the other one. So I have no clue where he's at.", I said with concern.

"You need me to come by?" he asked.

"No, no — don't worry. His phone is probably dead and forgot a charger. I'll let you know once I get in touch with him," I stated in an exasperated tone. I hung up. I thought to myself, "ok... we have Onstar — let me call them to see if they can find the car." I called them and they told me the account was not activated and that if I am concerned to call my local Sheriff's office. So I did. Approximately 10 mins later, Bob shows up. And 5 minutes after that — Hillsborough County Sheriff's Department shows up. She, the officer, is asking me all kinds of questions and if I think he would harm himself. I said, "Well, his son just passed away, so the likelihood is high, but I don't think he'd do anything crazy like that."

She asked me if she could look around, and I said "ok." She goes upstairs, and I end up talking to Bob downstairs in the kitchen. I honestly don't recall what we talked about because my mind was somewhere else completely. The officer comes back downstairs and tells me she's going to step outside. She came back in and asked, "Do you both mind coming outside with me?"

We look at each other and say "sure." As she closed the door, she just looked at me, and I asked "He's upstairs isn't he?" Her response is "yes".

I could say that I knew it, I could say I was mad... honestly, I could say a lot of things that day and in the months and years following that day. One thing is for sure, that day changed who I am as a person. I appreciate my relationships more than I did before. I have been doing a lot of energy healing. For me, traditional therapies were not something I could actually sit through. I am healing every day, and every day is completely different. When dealing with the overdose of a stepchild and the suicide of your husband, you view the world in a different light. People ask me a lot if I was or am angry with Dirk for doing this to me and to our family. My answer is, "I am not angry, but I was disappointed." Disappointed that I was not able to "fix" it, but now I realize that he didn't do this to me- this is something that happened in our lives because of his pain and sadness.

I began a blog to empower myself. It's taken me four years and I did it publicly for accountability for myself, but if I am able to speak to someone who is in the same boat as me and we can talk about how it feels when we're on the outside looking in, then I am ok with that. I was never exposed to this before, and I want to help people who are experiencing this currently, or have in the past, recognize different avenues to move forward and heal.

About the Author

STEPHANIE OLIVO

Stephanie Olivo-Schulte is an American entrepreneur and a Tampa, FL native. She has been a realtor since 2018. In 2017, after the suicide of her husband and the overdose of her stepson, she closed the doors. Olivo-Schulte decided to take these tragedies and begin a blog, "Discontinued, Now What?!", where she discusses the path she is now on. Her chapter in the newest installation from Inspired Hearts Publishing, The Voyage & The Return: The Path to Self-Discovery, takes a small peek into the day her late husband took his life.

Unhappy with traditional therapy, she was introduced to Reiki and meditation. This has helped her open her heart and mind to be able to aid women on their path after the suicide of a spouse. She wants to use this pain in dealing with depression, addiction, and suicide from an outsider's perspective to help others in similar situations.

website: www.dcnw.info

CHAPTER 13

You Are Not Crazy, You're Connected

VALERIA MARITZA

As I lay my head on the pillow, pretending to be asleep, I caught a glimpse of him completely immersed in what seemed to be an exciting and joyful conversation with someone online.

We had managed to tie the knot just two months before my mom's passing. She battled a fast-moving form of breast cancer, and we lost her barely 18 months from the day of her diagnosis. The grief of losing her brought me down a fast deep spiral that I could no longer control. I was so depressed, hopeless, and felt as if there was no one to talk to. I bought myself a sketchbook, and I started to "talk" to it on my long train ride to work. It was really bad. I would begin to write in my book, and rivers of tears would helplessly flow down my cheeks. I didn't know where to hide my face. I would choose a seat by the window, hoping I could bury my face to the side and that no one would notice, holding on to any muffled cries that might want to be fully expressed. I am sure people just politely looked the other way and left me alone, as I repeated this behavior day in and day out on the same train, at the same time, with the same people.

My writing became my savior. I felt heard and seen and was able to put on a fake happy face with family, friends, and colleagues, after writing in that book. But inside, I was still dying. I knew there was something else going on.

And so came that night when I noticed him looking at the screen and **I just knew**. You know, that feeling that comes in, where you just know what's going on? I lay there trying to figure out how I could get up and reach him before he could close the conversation. I failed. He quickly rid himself of any clues and denied any wrongdoing, **but I knew**.

That was the beginning of the end. What I should have known for years before was finally unfolding to its undeniable destiny. They say you can take the short and sweet way to your joyful life destination, or you can choose to take the long way home. I had taken the long and painful way home. The feelings, the messages, the items found, the experiences and knowings that were felt deep in my gut, were all pointing to let me know I was on the wrong path with this person, yet I continued to deny them. And so the universe finally gave me this ultimatum, of facing my deepest fears with absolutely no more patience.

In a whirlwind, he left our home without ever saying a word. He avoided all my phone calls and just refused to talk. I was incredibly confused, hurt, and filled with questions I needed to be answered in order to be able to understand what had happened and how we got here in the first place. But it was useless. I was successfully dodged for what felt to be about 2 months. Can you imagine what goes on in one's mind without answers for that long? During this time, it also became clear that the people I considered my dear friends were actually not. No one wanted to take sides, and no one offered any answers. I was looked at as the one who had "done something wrong" and needed to be avoided, adding even more to my confusion. I felt every piece of information, and words of comfort were laced with doubts about my own integrity. They didn't say these things, but I could feel them!

When I didn't know where to find my then-husband to get answers, everyone else knew where he was but didn't offer to say. I found out at one point that I was being blamed for things I hadn't done! All it took was one person, the one who was betraying me, to say something about me that wasn't true, for everyone to believe him and doubt me. Didn't they know me? Didn't they know my character and what I was all about? Was one simple lie all it took for my entire reputation to be doubted? This was the lowest of the blows. I felt so alone and let down by the people I knew and was close to in my life. I wanted to die. I sat on my kitchen floor holding a huge sharp knife while breaking down and crying because I was too "chicken" to even hurt myself. I was stuck.

Being raised Roman Catholic, this was the worst thing that could have happened. I was failing at one of the "laws" that had been instilled in me all of my life! I couldn't give up on my marriage! How could I go on? What would people think of me? Would I become part of the statistics?

I was losing weight rapidly as I could not get anything down my throat. Even on a seemingly good day, when I thought I was feeling better and my favorite foods were offered to me (homemade chicken cutlets by my ex's Italian mom), I found myself fully intending to eat, and literally not being able to put the food in my mouth.

Have you ever felt that type of grief, where your body is so disconnected from your soul and broken from the inside out? This is what it can feel like. In that moment, I realized my wounds were so much deeper than I was allowing myself to believe, for the purposes of being strong and putting on a good face. I wanted to look as if I had it together and was going to get through my trauma even though I was still in the midst of the chaos. Does anyone relate? My mom raised a strong woman who wouldn't need a man to make her whole, and this I was determined to prove. But I had failed at demonstrating this too.

Soon, I realized our first year anniversary was approaching, and as I saw no changes in anything pertaining to where or why my relationship had disintegrated, I decided that it would be up to me to make a change. *I decided in one moment that I could either continue waiting for someone else to "save me", feeling sorry for myself, or do something about it that would bring me joy.* And so, I chose joy.

I decided to book a solo trip to Italy exactly during the week that was to be my one-year anniversary. I was not going to sit at home thinking of what it could have been, wondering what he might be doing, or what my friends would be thinking about me, or if they would try to comfort me all the while not being totally honest with me. Making this single decision gave me strength and joy. Something I could look forward to.

It was a sunny, cool afternoon when I boarded the airport bus from NYC. I sat by the window with my one suitcase and backpack when all of sudden, fear and doubt began to fill my body. Since I was traveling alone, I had no one to lean on for support. I nervously took out my 14 x 11 sketchbook that I had purchased with the intention of drawing all the beautiful places I would soon be seeing, and instead, began to write.

"What was I doing? Was I crazy to take a big international trip all by myself? What would I do all alone there? This was a bad idea. Maybe I should just go back home and not get on that plane."

Writing these sentences down seemed to be working at calming me down and giving me something to do to keep my mind and body busy. I began to "talk" with my mom. It felt as if she could hear my thoughts as I wrote them down, and I could hear her answers in my head. The emotional turmoil released some tears that quickly rolled down my cheek. I had flashbacks of the time when I was hiding my face on the train on my way to work, and I nervously searched for a tissue to clean myself up. The writing took about a page and then ceased on its own. The process had brought me peace, and I now felt calm, centered, and excited about my trip again.

The feeling of adventure carried me all the way from the airport, to the plane, to my destination in Italy. My fears, disappointment, and sadness vanished and were replaced by the beautiful views I saw from the sky, the surprising meals I was served on the plane (they had ice cream!), the new movies I got to watch, and the total immersion of everyone's joyful energy who was traveling with me on that flight. Once we landed, I focused on finding my way to the train that would take me to Venice and then on my walk through the cobblestone streets up to my hotel.

I checked in the lobby of a quaint little place right in the middle of a busy street. My room was on the second floor and had an ornate balcony with a view of the street I had just walked on. You could see and hear the multitude of people walking right below in such close proximity that we could make eye contact, and the fear set in again. Without so much as a plan of what I would actually do once I had arrived here, I felt, for the first time, afraid and completely out of place. I took out my sketchbook once again and wrote in it all my feelings and doubts, as if the book was listening to me. It worked again! I don't even know why at this point I was still surprised by this, but I was.

I succumbed to sleep after my long trip, and when I awoke, my fears were gone. In the evening, I took a stroll exploring this beautiful city. The water and the gondolas were just as romantic as they are portrayed in the movies. The old streets curved gracefully, leading you up and down the steps to various bridges, revealing a new church at every turn. I arrived at Piazza San Marco close to sunset and was welcomed with a view that was so splendid I could never forget it. The mosaics on St. Marc's Basilica were glistening in brilliant gold light that seemed as if it was painted with a smooth brush stroke. That was a view that could only be seen when the sun was reflecting just right on the walls. I was not aware of this phenomenon, or of how lucky I had been to have witnessed it. I realized this later when I went back several times to the same spot, only to see the beauty of the architecture without the golden splendor. This realization made me feel alive, inspired, and protected by a power so much greater than I.

The miracles continued to unfold the next day when I took a boat ride across the water to a beautiful small white-domed basilica called Salute. I entered the domed area and sat down on one of the benches near the center, closed my eyes, and suddenly, I could hear my mom's voice, clear as if she was sitting right next to me. We had this beautiful, strong exchange of words that happened telepathically but felt like a normal conversation between two live people. I could feel my tears rolling down my cheeks again. My face was facing upwards and I didn't dare open my eyes for fear of disconnecting from this divine connection. My mom told me how proud she was of me for the decisions I had made and the actions I had taken to turn my life around. She also gave me messages to share with both my brother and sister, and we talked about my dad, who was then still alive. It was the most gratifying, loving experience I have ever had. When we said goodbye, I opened my eyes and the transmission ceased. People were staring at me as they walked silently past my bench. I was completely unaware of anyone else being in that space with me. What had just happened? I didn't know. I didn't question. I just knew it had been real, and I was ecstatic.

Two days later, I was on another train on my way to Rome. I walked to see many tourist places, including the Spanish Steps, where I climbed all the way up and found, you guessed it, another church. Inside, there was a wedding in process, so I found a niche to the side where I intended to wait, and there I met a Spanish priest. What are the chances of that? I felt called to tell him my story and ask for advice. He listened and offered that I should seek an annulment. This, my friends, is nothing less than my third miracle. The heaviest part that was downing on me was the "failure of marriage" because of my upbringing beliefs in my faith. And here was this priest in Rome, speaking my native language, telling me to get an annulment. I felt so relieved and took this as a direct sign from God, who was giving me the green light to dissolve my marriage, with His full support and forgiveness.

I came back home full of determination and with a clear plan as to what I needed to do. First, I looked for a lawyer and filed for divorce. Then, I was able to receive a resolution of divorce, begin the complicated trail of paperwork for my annulment, find a new home for most of my belongings, sell my house, and move to live full time in Italy, all within the next four months. I had lost everything as I knew it, yet I felt so full of direction and with a new purpose for life. I was finally living my life the way I wanted to live it, doing all the things I loved to do, like dancing, traveling, sightseeing, creating art, and making new friends. I took several other solo trips to visit Spain and France and visited many museums and beautiful places. I realized that the end of my marriage had created space and freedom to live my life as I wanted without needing to get approval from anyone! As a matter of fact, had it not been for my short marriage, I would have still felt as if I needed to ask permission from my father in order to move forward. But as I had already left my house to form my adult life, I felt in charge of it and independent. You see, it had to have happened this way. It was all divinely planned.

After nine months of living in paradise, I decided to come back to the States to work for a few months, save some money, and then return to my freestyle living in Italy. I chose to move to Nashville, where my sister was living, so I could spend some time with her. That was the year the Twin Towers fell, and as the world closed down, I never went back.

Life in Nashville was a great slow exploration for me. I became immersed in yoga, meditation, and healing practices. I constantly sought out the advice of different mediums and psychics. And then something interesting began to occur. Some friends of mine would call me at random times and ask me if I could help them with something like a headache, and I would say yes, place my hands on my forehead, and begin to feel their pain in my body, and then they would say their pain was gone. I didn't think anything of this. I don't know why they asked me, or why I said yes. I don't know how I did it, or what I did. And so, I just labeled those events as "play" and didn't talk or think twice about them.

Nashville was also the place I met my current husband. We met at the perfect time for both of our lives, and I attribute this meeting to divine guidance and intervention. We created a beautiful family, and I had everything I always wanted, but something started to bug me.

You know the saying "it's not the destination, but the journey"? Once I had achieved all I thought I wanted, I still felt there was something missing. I had been chasing only the dreams I was told I should have, not the ones that were bubbling inside. I had the love of my life, a beautiful child, a career, a home, health, a car; what else was there?

I was feeling comfortable in the everyday routine, but with an incessant feeling inside that there was something else bigger, that I needed to explore. I began to purposely look within and trust my intuition. This led me to find support to guide me on my journey. Once I began to pay attention to what my gut was saying, everything began to make sense. I started to make connections all the way back to my childhood. My gifts and abilities came flooding out and became incredibly active. I was connected all along; I was just not listening! And just like when you pick up a bike after years of not riding one, and all the skills come back to you instantly as you begin to remember, I started to ride my wave of trust and sovereignty. Remembering who I truly was before the conditioning started.

My story of dissolution began over 20 years ago, and embodying my purpose was unnecessarily drawn out. I was living my life by pleasing others and playing small for the purpose of making everyone else around me feel comfortable. And in doing so, I ended up betraying and losing myself.

I share my story because I know so many will be able to see themselves in it, in not following their gut feelings, inner knowing and intuition. And, maybe reading this story can collapse your time in becoming whole.

About the Author
VALERIA MARITZA

Valeria is a Quantum Energy Healer, Intuitive Psychic Medium, Akashic Records, Reiki Healer, and Light Language Queen! She has helped dozens of people heal and transform their lives by targeting deep healing transformations, guiding them through a journey to remember who they truly are, and shining their true divine selves unapologetically.

Valeria Maritza, previously known as Valeria Maritza Olivos, has been a free-spirited wild child since the beginning. Never resonating with man-made rules and constrictions or formalities, she decided to use both her first and middle names as her legal name, so as to avoid anyone calling her by a formal last name.

Valeria is the host of the *Healing Through You podcast* and the founder of *Dream Weaving You*, a four-month journey of transformation. She's a channeled artist, bringing the divine through her free-hand mandala paintings.

Valeria works with the Angels and the energy of Love, which is the highest frequency used in all her healings and transmissions.

Valeria has taught the abstracts of visual art for over 15 years and brings this deep knowledge of being able to see her students where they are and understanding their modes of learning to her business, making it really easy to relate and teach content in a way that her clients can best receive it.

Valeria holds a BFA and an MS in art education.

Valeria was born in Chile, grew up in New York, and has traveled to many parts of the world.

Valeria is a wife and a mother to a beautiful ray of light 6-year-old son.

Connect with Valeria:

On her website : www.healingthroughyou.com

Instagram: www.instagram.com/vale_5358

Healing Through You Podcast: *www.podcasts.apple.com/us/podcast/healing-through-you/id1607878246*

CHAPTER 14

Wandering Woman at Heart

RUTH ANN KRISA

Have you been a *WANDERING WOMAN AT HEART*?

We are all *WANDERING WOMEN AT HEART* as we have all walked a path of others' dreams.

How many paths has your SOUL taken?

Is your SOUL telling you that you are destined to do something just out of your grasp?

At 7 years old, I knew I was different but had no words to describe why.

At 13, I began to understand what type of "different" I was.

At 66, I have walked a path of being different and also a path of trying to fit in.

Is it TIME you look at *your* SOUL'S existence?

Answer this question.

My soul is _____.

My thoughts are bound by the ties I have to the earth's rotation.

All of the rotations make my body grow wiser and I ponder where my soul will land.

If we could look back at each rotation we have taken, would we be able to pluck one memory to hang on the clothesline that is our life?

OR has your SOUL lived someone else's desire? Would each of those memories change where we are today?

My rotations are _____.

My soul is _____.

In my mind, I am _____.

My body feels _____.

How many rotations do you wish you existed in?

How many rotations do you think you have left?

How many rotations do you feel completed in?

If your SOUL'S journey comes to you in the night, is it real? OR is it just a dream you have been thinking about for a long time?

WE ARE HERE TO TELL STORIES. As life is created, so are stories. Each of us has walked the path of our story, and we get to choose the stories we share.

The reflections that follow were created while I slept. As I woke up, all of these words were flowing through my mind. I got up and wrote them down, not knowing what I was going to be doing with them.

I believe my mind has been creating these SOUL PURPOSE moments so I could share them with others.

As a *WANDERING WOMAN AT HEART,* who has felt that they are never seen?

I am nobody. I am somebody.

I am the soul of a nobody left behind and I am the soul that somebody found.

I am the nobody people stare through; I am the somebody people stop and stare at.

What could I have become if I was a somebody? I will never know as I am a nobody.

Life gives the somebodies a purpose and a plan.

As a nobody, life lets you meander on your own with the hopes of finding a path.

If a somebody and a nobody connect, they may create an anybody.

But the chances of that happening are left to the consequences of the universe.

As a *WANDERING WOMAN AT HEART,* who has felt her **SOUL ROOTS** grow?

Our journey begins without our **SOUL** knowing.

Our **SOUL ROOTS** grow toward a life.

As we are nourished, our **SOUL** grows.

Some of us receive less **SOUL ROOTS** than others.

Some of us receive all the ingredients of loving **SOUL ROOTS**.

But we, as **SOUL ROOTS,** can expand our nourishment as we move along our journey of life.

As a *WANDERING WOMAN AT HEART,* who has felt they were a door blowing in the wind?

Promises spoken through unbroken Doors.

You promised me laughter.

You promised me love.

You said you would love me, till I was old and worn.

But now you have gone off with a new shiny shadow.

Promises spoken but silenced as dark and thick as the night.

The heart is broken.

No more unbroken doors.

You left my heart as shattered as the glass, torn as the screen and closed when you left.

As a *WANDERING WOMAN AT HEART,* who has looked through a window wishing you were on the other side?

How Many Windows do you have to look through?

Do you ever feel that your life is a window that looks out at others, and you keep waiting for your ray of Sunshine?

As you move into the next chapter of your life, remember there are rays of sunshine, but you might have to look out a different window.

As you continue to look out your window, remember your shade is drawing shut. Is it time to look out a different window to see your rays of sunshine?

As a WANDERING WOMAN AT HEART, are you a woman of many dreams?

Have your dreams been fueled by the encounters of souls you have touched?

As a *WANDERING WOMAN AT HEART,* it doesn't matter if your dream is in a small recess of your heart, or if you are ready to step into a dream of a lifetime.

As a *WANDERING WOMAN AT HEART,* maybe you have had your boots on and have been stomping around for more years than you care to share... Now is your time to become a *WANDERING WOMAN AT HEART that can accomplish your dreams and find your* **SOUL ROOTS** *so you can grow into the* **WOMAN** *you know you are.*

About the Author
RUTH ANN KRISA

Ruth Ann Krisa proclaims, "I am a Wandering Woman at Heart who has walked a path of other's dreams."

At 7 years old, she knew she was different but had no words to describe why.

At 13, she began to understand what type of "difference" she was.

At 66, she has walked a path of being different and trying to fit in.

She lives in Southern California with her wife and dogs.

All of the reflections in her chapter came to her when she woke in the middle of the night. She knew they needed to be shared.

As she looks for the path she was supposed to take, she hopes these reflections help guide others through their purpose and journey. She hopes the reflections help others to see that there are many other paths that can be taken.

Connect with and follow

Ruth Ann Krisa on Facebook

https://www.facebook.com/groups/3221162901458115

By Email: ww.at.heart@gmail.com

CHAPTER 15

Through Darkness Comes Light

ASHLEY SHELDON-GATES

There I was stepping out of a much-needed hot shower, naked and alone, preparing for yet another morning as I faced myself in the mirror. As I swiped my hand gently across the chilled, fogged-up mirror, I immediately noticed something was different. My morning routine usually consisted of me picking apart every inch of myself, or more commonly, looking past myself entirely in hopes of avoiding the person looking back. Small, tender red bumps would outline my forehead down to my jawline. Dark blue puffy bags weighed down my sad and tired eyes. Unruly freckles scattered across my face like stars in a summer sky, while an array of discolorations imprinted upon my pale white skin. To my surprise, this was not what caught my attention that morning; instead I found myself staring mysteriously back into my glossed over icy-blue eyes and deep into my soul. After a minute had passed, a feeling of warmth grazed down my damp, cold body, as if the sun was piercing in through the window behind me. Tears began to fill my eyes and, like an overflowing river in spring, rushed down my cheeks, washing away the freckles for a brief moment. My legs began to tremble, and my knees buckled as I dropped to the hard bathroom floor. I did not see the usual imperfections I tended to focus on when faced with my reflection each day. Nor was it the covered up version that most people, including myself, knew best. This time, I saw past the surface and an overwhelming feeling of love and acceptance took over. The shame and sorrow were melting away, and gratitude was proudly taking their place. Confused with what I had felt, I stood back up to take another look, and there I was, an imperfect beautiful being radiating with compassion and understanding for myself. A brave, resilient woman who had finally overcome the most challenging season. The scars would always remain, but I was standing.

To help you understand what led up to this moment, I will take you back to the spring of 2016. My husband and I were in over our heads in debt following the crash of 2008. We had spent years trying to dig ourselves out of financial instability, only to find ourselves deeper in the hole. Due to a rather difficult upbringing, these hard times in my adult life caused my anxiety to re-emerge and lead me back to living in my emotional home of isolation; one of constant fear and worry. After a long seven-year battle of living paycheck to paycheck and emptying the coin jar to get us by, we were desperate for a miracle. So, I made a choice, with the encouragement of my husband, to enter into a career I had no prior knowledge of. I made a decision that day to devote my everything to changing the course of direction for my family. With no college education, no degrees in business or any prior experience, I pushed myself to learn the skills needed to succeed. I would spend hours upon hours on personal development and becoming my best self. My sole focus was to overcome adversity and set the greatest example for my children. I was determined to make my family proud; I was ready to give us a life worth living, one I knew we deserved. To my greatest surprise, we quickly built a global team as I went above and beyond to serve them on every level. I grew into a leader who guided other women and encouraged them to gain control of their lives. In our first year, we cultivated a large community of like minded individuals who worked together courageously building a legacy for our families. The unexpected growth I proved, and at such a quick speed, afforded me the opportunity to be scouted for my advice and knowledge amongst my peers and other leaders. Suddenly, people were looking to me for advice and career advancement, which felt like a blessing and a curse all at the same time. It was great to be needed and seen, something I hadn't experienced before, but with that also came an overwhelming need to be perfect. I felt an immense amount of pressure to carry myself in a certain way in hopes of gaining even more approval from others. I was vulnerable about our financial struggle, sharing my story publicly and lightly touching on my history of anxiety. Never going too deep on that subject, mostly because I hadn't taken the time to really uncover it for myself. At this point, though, what did it matter? I was feeling better than ever as I felt accepted and valued in my career.

In the summer of 2019, another opportunity arose which would take me by surprise. I was very devoted to the product I was promoting, but beyond that, I was even more so devoted to the people I worked with. I tried to ignore the feelings that something was wrong and remain focused on where I was, but after a few months passed, my gut was telling me my time there was complete. I couldn't stop thinking about the new products revealed to me, the company's mission, and how their core values aligned with my every being. I made the hardest decision that June, to walk away from all I had built, heading blindly into the unknown once again and starting over. It was a difficult decision, but I was confident it would further my career, our team's success, and our financial futures. After my decision was made, a powerful lesson would follow about friendships and living for others. I was very unprepared for the harsh opinions and criticism that would follow. Many of my friends would support me and were happy to see my growth and advancement. On the other hand, there were also a few who were very offended by my decision and rather blunt about it too. Women that I had previously given my everything to, began ridiculing me and unfriending me for bettering my family. I was speechless with how quickly I went from the most selfless, kind, loving leader who would do anything for anyone, to a "trader" and a "liar." I was disgusted and heartbroken seeing so many true colors revealed. All those years, loving and supporting these women, to later be met with such hatred, was an eye-opening moment for me. I was being exposed to some of the worst parts of humanity first hand. I couldn't wrap my head around being angry with someone for trying to better their lives; it just made no sense to me. Although my soul was rattled by their actions and hurtful words, I knew I had made the right decision for my family and tried to keep my attention there. The first week of transitioning was hard to say the least, but I kept telling myself, "You have no choice but to succeed." Within the first three months, myself and much of the team were quickly climbing the ranks, surpassing where we were in previous years. It was incredible to witness and confirmed that the decision we made was the right one. We were proud to be standing together and stronger than ever! Since our team took off running, I never really had much time to pay any more attention to the hurt and betrayal I had experienced upon my exit. I had to keep my chin up and keep a strong exterior.

That was until 2020 arrived with a world-shaking virus. I'm sure this is easily a time many of us can recall and feel the fear and uncertainty. I was coming off of the biggest year of my career as I was still very fresh in my transition into the health and wellness realm. Our team was growing at a rapid speed once again, exceeding expectations and achieving advancements left and right. To top it off, the company announced a new product that would be launching the following year that would grant us even more success. I was in my prime, or so I thought. It was a Tuesday evening and we had just finished up dinner when my phone alerted me that our local schools would be following suit with many other districts around the world and begin implementing distance learning. Overnight, my kitchen became my children's classroom, and it is where I'd play the role of teacher for the next few months. It would start out as a fun game of pretend or, even better, a vacation from our busy, over-committed schedules. We unknowingly joked that it was an answer to our prayers, giving us a chance to finally slow down. It wasn't until the school year ended and summer was in full force that things really began sinking in. I became exhausted and inundated in a state of overwhelm. Work events, vacations, self-care appointments, and luncheons were quickly coming to a halt, canceled one by one. Social media, being the main platform for my business, was growing more toxic by the day. Immersed in negative opinions, closed minds, hatred, and strong political views made it rather difficult to show up and be present like I needed to. Everything around me was quickly becoming chaotic, and the world seemed to be growing darker and darker. Each day that passed in quarantine would push another buried wound up to the surface, reminding me it was there and unhealed. I would quickly reject the feeling and sweep it back under the rug where I felt it belonged. By this point in my life, I had become a pro at numbing what I didn't want to feel and concealing it with a big smile. July came in, shaking the ground beneath me, bringing sad news of the loss of a dear family member. My structured façade was crumbling apart, and playing pretend, masking the pain, was becoming a bigger challenge. I was growing weaker by the day, suffocating in my anxiety and depression. For months, I had been telling myself it would pass, but the more I tried to ignore it, the worse it got. I remember days feeling selfish for achieving all that I had and not being able to find an ounce of joy inside of me. We had come so far, and now I was being faced with feelings I hadn't felt in years. Being stuck at home for so many months with nowhere to run off to was causing everything inside me to rebel. I was sad, angry, confused, and completely lost. I could feel the light inside of me dimming, and any care to be alive was almost nonexistent. Each breath I took brought more pain, and most mornings I woke up finding myself wishing I hadn't. The racing thoughts, heavy chest, emptiness, and feeling of sadness had overpowered my entire being. I had lost all hope again and was unsure if I could ever get it back.

November of 2020 arrived and brought with it a new career opportunity for my husband this time. He has always been my biggest supporter over the years and believed in me more than I ever did myself. For as long as I can remember, he always dreamt of running his own business and here it was. We knew he could not pass up the chance to see it through, even with the big risks. He would have to make a decision to walk away from a steady job, a consistent paycheck, and benefits for our family. As if that wasn't enough, committing to the gamble would also require us to uproot our family six hours away. After many prayers pleading for unmistakable signs and many tears, we made the gut-wrenching decision to relocate our family and move away from the town we called home for the past twelve years. I was still at an all-time low, and here we were heading out into the unknown in the middle of a pandemic. I was worried; however, the change of scenery sounded a bit refreshing for my troubled mind. On the fifth of December, we set out on our new adventure and, with heavy hearts, said our goodbyes. I'd be lying if I said everything fell into place upon our arrival in Southern Utah, but it was actually the exact opposite of that. Finding a home in the housing crisis was a headache all in itself, and once we did, it took most of our savings to make the home even livable. After three months of renovating, living on concrete floors, and out of the garage, we slowly began settling into our new home.

February approached without delay, and my company's annual conference was on the books. Due to the pandemic still lingering amongst us, it would be changed to a virtual event this year. Disappointed to not be able to see our team in person also came with the relief of not having to reveal my gloomy state. The following week, I'd receive an invitation to attend a small in-person gathering with a local team to watch the conference together. I was hesitant to accept being I was still not feeling like myself, but after much consideration, I decided to go. I had been isolating myself for months now and knew deep down that what I needed was human connection. I forced myself to attend that weekend and, thank God, I did. The first day I was extremely nervous due to my struggles with anxiety and, to add in, the fact that I didn't know very many people there. That night, those women would help me break down some massive walls and gain clarity on why I had felt so broken. Some shared their stories as well, and I quickly realized I wasn't alone in feeling the way that I had. We cried together, laughed together, and, best of all, we grew together. Day two of the retreat was another big day for me. I vividly remember waking up that morning, stepping out of that hot shower and feeling blessed to be alive. The feeling of gratitude taking over had seemed like it had been missing for an eternity. This was also the day our company would announce the new product everyone had been waiting for. It had been in the works for years and was the first of its kind, which brought major excitement. Little did I know that this retreat, those women, and that product would be the catalyst for my healing journey. For the first time in my life, I felt that I belonged somewhere and I didn't have to change myself to be accepted by them. Sadly, this also made me realize a common pattern amongst many women, one of belonging and conforming to what society tells us we should be. My eyes were now opening to the fact that I had spent most of my life measuring my worth by how others viewed me. I had wasted so much of my life seeking validation and fighting for acceptance. I left that retreat a new person with a big purpose to continue helping women but in a more significant way. More empowering than financial security, recognition, and the likes of strangers. My new mission was to encourage a belief system and an understanding of self-acceptance.

Over the next few months, I would practice mindfulness, journaling, meditation, breathwork, and improve my brain health with dietary adjustments and other alternative medicines. I would read books, listen to podcasts, and follow life coaches trying to learn all I could in order to uncover where this programming was rooted from. My quest eventually led me to a local spiritual community, which magnified my awakening. In these sessions, I would begin uncovering some daunting memories from my younger years and understand the only way to live out my purpose was to heal first. Many memories I had blocked out entirely, and reliving those traumas from a new perspective was the only way through them. The mind is a powerful vessel, and mine tried to protect me by forgetting those difficult times, but the trauma was still trapped deep inside my body. I believe God places us exactly where we're supposed to be and nothing in this life happens by accident or chance. I know all the challenges I faced as a child, during my career transition, through the pandemic and our relocation, led me to exactly where I am supposed to be today. I am confident our trials are laid before us to elevate us to the next level, and when we are knocked off the path, it's to save us from unhealthy relationships and environments that are no longer serving us. I had to redefine success from what had been taught to me by my peers and society. Success is not the amount of followers you have or how many people have stopped to view your last post on social media. Success is not your titles, your degrees, the size of your paycheck, or the amount of money sitting in your bank account. Success is living a fulfilled life and not allowing the opinions of others to determine how that should look. It's listening to your own inner-voice, knowing your core beliefs, and living aligned with your values. Success is being your raw and authentic self. It is taking back your power from those who've rejected and abandoned you along the way. Success is stepping into who you are meant to be, no longer dimming your light to fit inside someone else's box. Success is being brave and vulnerable, asking for support when we know we need it most. I would have never learned what really matters if it wasn't for the pandemic forcing me to face myself. I share this part of my story in the hopes that you see healing is a voyage that is possible and worth it. We are not meant to live stuck in our struggles, so give yourself permission to break free. The only obstacle is you, and it's only through the darkness that we can find our light. Today you may feel lost, but trust that it's God's way of redirecting you to a greater path designed for the return home to yourself.

About the Author
ASHLEY SHELDON-GATES

Ashley Sheldon is a dedicated mother, a self-made entrepreneur and a devoted wife. She currently lives in Southern Utah with her husband and two beautiful children. She is proud to be living life on purpose. She was called on six years ago to support a start-up company where she promoted a new revolutionary product. Despite self doubt and a lack of prior experience, Ashley took on the role and launched a large successful team that quickly climbed to the top. Three years later her passion elevated and she began studying Health and Wellness with the intent of understanding true healing from the inside-out. Using her phone and social media, Ashley rose to the occasion and brought together many like minded souls to build a global winning team. Ashley believes her greatest achievement is watching everyday people, especially moms, gain back control of their lives. It is an honor for Ashley to help others become leaders and she is passionate about supporting them in creating a life they've always dreamed of. Ashley is a warrior for humanity and leads her life with kindness.

With the upheaval in 2020 Ashley found herself battling severe anxiety and depression. She sought out on a journey for deep healing and self discovery. This was a brutal fight digging into the blocked and unhealed parts of her soul, but walking through that darkness is where she found her light. Ashley knows her creator has placed her in this exact moment in time to be a beacon for other women who may have also let their light burn out along the way. She believes we are all forever students in this ever changing world and in that same breath, we are also teachers, here to guide one another as we progress through life.

Ashley is passionate about humanity & helping others heal from the inside out.

Find out how you can work with her here: https://linktr.ee/ashley_sheldon_gates

Connect on Facebook:
www.facebook.com/ashley.sheldon.79

Connect on Instagram:
www.instagram.com/ashley_sheldon_gates

CHAPTER 16

Dreaming over Blank Pages

REBEKAH MEREDITH

I have been staring at a black page for most of my life. I've written pages and chapters for anyone else who would grace me. If I wrote anything for myself, I would cover it up with white ink. A story hiding in plain sight, begging to be read, wanting to be acknowledged, but always silent. Countless hours have been spent staring at empty pages while I imagined what they could potentially hold. I spent years dreaming of the possibilities but never actually doing anything. And if I did do anything, I got scared and abandoned the ship — hiding evidence of anything started out of fear.

Why did I let this happen?

Abused?... Tiny scribbles in white ink.

Raped?... Tears covered blank pages in silence.

Near-death?... Words were written but not spoken, and black ink turned white.

My words... my voice... were covered up and shushed. Why? Because it's been ingrained in me for years by many that feeling grief is a sign of weakness. It's been carved into my soul that my emotions are invalid. It's been beaten into my heart that if I experience suffering, I deserve it in some way.

Why? What did I do?

I hardened myself from the inside out to never show my emotions, to hide my emotions, and to silence my trauma. My walls were built with the toughest material, and my soul was hidden by white ink. But alas, my walls had a tiny crack. My inner being longed for someone to see me and help me color pages.

Most of my walls started breaking down when I met the true love of my life, my husband. He saw the true me begging to be seen and heard. And when those walls broke, there was still white ink. But, there was also a scared child who was relieved that she was finally being seen. Days turned to weeks, weeks to months, months to years, and in time, the black pages I saw every day turned from white to grey. An outline was forming, and a structure was being made.

Over time, I gained the strength to add color to my pages. I still, however, guarded my pages. My pages were bound in a white cover to blend with the white pages the world saw when they looked at me. I didn't want anyone to know. I, myself, did not want to know. Or at least, I thought I didn't.

Over many years and with lots of patience, my husband helped me learn truths about myself and awaken forgotten memories from traumatic years prior to him. It's funny how our own minds protect us from trauma by forgetting, or at least burying truths deep within ourselves. More and more truths came out, and more outlines were made in my pages, but the outlines were still not filled. This was something I had to do on my own.

The first step in not using white ink anymore was having someone show me that I didn't need to hide. The next step, and the hardest, was convincing myself to go over the white ink with colors. I didn't know where to start since most of my mind hid my memory. I spent a long time in the dark staring at nothing and trying to figure out what my next move would be. I stayed in this spot until I got pregnant. That's when things got worse, and progress was undone.

The outlines were still there, but I didn't recognize them anymore. The white ink didn't take back the outlines. Instead, they made the pages harder to look at. I couldn't see beyond anything and fell into prenatal depression on top of clinical depression. My senses were messed up, my energy levels tanked, and my willpower emptied to almost nothing. I remained in this state for thirty-seven weeks and five days. At this time, I went into labor and was not ready to be a mother. I endured a day and a half of grueling pain, wishing for it to just be over!

When we neared the end of my torment while waiting for my baby to be born, there was a shift. And once again, I was told to write with white ink as nurses pinned me down and told me to fight my body's urge to push. I did as I was told because it came so naturally to me. I had to. My baby's life was at risk. Every ounce of my physical being told me to push, but I couldn't. My baby would die if I did. I fought it. I cried. I prayed for the torment to end! And then everything went black. There was a tiny bit of silver as I saw myself dead and a doctor yanking my baby out of my temporarily lifeless body. It was a second, but it felt like an eternity as I watched and wondered what would happen if I did not survive. I couldn't leave my husband behind. I couldn't let him write in white ink or leave our child to face a similar path.

That second was long, but it was the second that changed my life and showed me color.

Despite near death, despite depression — old and new — I endured. I only saw colored blurs for the next few months as I navigated motherhood for the first time. The clear white was so tempting, but I knew it would only make my depression worse. And I couldn't do that to my husband and child. That one second resonated with me and still does.

It took near death and wanting to live for those I love, those who I don't want to see suffer, to transform into a strong being without walls and without using white ink to silence myself. The journey is not over. On the contrary, the journey is becoming clearer as the blurs sharpen into fine lines and as I can finally start to see the words I wrote in white turn to color. My pages are now not so blank, and I dream of the day I finally get to let them shine.

About the Author

REBEKAH MEREDITH

Rebekah Meredith is a wife, mother, blogger, and author. She spends her days enjoying the little things with her family. At night, she works on building her dream of spreading mental health awareness through her writing.

Her chapter *Dreaming over Blank Pages* is an intimate look into the layers of writer's block and mental health. Rebekah's background in psychology has helped her bring blocks into a new light and shine awareness on them. Seeing and understanding are two perspectives that often get confused when attempting to be aware. Separating the two helps us learn the how and why, while healing our blocks. Overcoming obstacles can go far beyond any page.

• Visit my website: www.rebekah-meredith.com

CHAPTER 17

The Inside Job

TANIA ORMONDE

It is our duty to shine our brightest light and elevate the vibration of the world! As fallen humans, we are broken but have the opportunity to be made whole again. Decluttering and organizing your person and personal space can aid and even fast-track your **journey to self-discovery** and enlightenment. The journey begins by taking a deep look and honing in on the purpose of your being, spirit, and belongings, with the intention of appreciating what value each has brought or brings to your life, identifying the items that no longer serve, and embracing what you are left with. **The process** of elimination takes us on a journey of self-discovery in understanding how we have become who we are through the items, thoughts, and emotions we hold on to. There is work to do! We are the **creators of our own universe,** but only because God created us in His image. We are born at our highest and purest vibration – I AM LOVE! Behold, the journey of life does taint our being. At some point, many of us realize that we must put in the work to reunite with our highest of beings. It is then that we decide that enough is enough and that it's time to **find the balance,** keep the best of the best and get rid of the rest. We are beings of vibration and therefore have the capacity to vibe at the frequency of our choosing, but we must commit to taking on the BIG challenge – THE INSIDE JOB!

Discovering who God has intended me to be has been the journey of a lifetime thus far! The most insightful has been the decade that led me into the 40ies! For the first five years of the last ten, I plunged right into everything. Diving in headfirst! Let me give you some context. I was born in Massachusetts into an immigrant family that fled to the United States looking for a promising future. I completed kindergarten in Terceira (an island in the Azores, Portugal). 1st, 2nd, and 3rd grade were completed at a bilingual school in Massachusetts. 3rd again, 4th, 5th, 6th, and 7th grade were completed in Graciosa (an island in the Azores, Portugal). 8th grade and beyond were completed back in Massachusetts! Many trips have taken place since this time; Canada, Mexico, Dominican Republic, most of the Caribbean islands, Portugal, Spain, France, Slovakia, Czech Republic, Turkey, Hungary, Austria, Russia, and Georgia to name a few. Following are some challenges that have contributed to my journey.

Shortly after receiving a scholarship to play collegiate soccer, I suffered an accident as a pedestrian. That night, I was informed that I was paralyzed from the neck down – but God had other plans for me. I would need motion to contribute goodness to the world. It was then that I understood how very precious the gift of life is. That is why it is called the PRESENT! After attending college and playing soccer for two years, my major was dropped. I came to a crossroads and decided to work while attending college, which led me to the "10-year plan." My higher education allowed me to break down some limiting beliefs I held near and dear, including that I was not independent, intelligent, or creative. My education in Cultural Geography enabled me to travel and appreciate that everyone everywhere is unique. **Besides being part of a country or a culture, each one of us brings a distinct energy that we get to gift to humanity. Let us not waste it!**

So much happened during the last ten years. Every experience is like a string being intertwined with such precision and beauty, an exquisite tapestry in the making! 30 to 40 a decade, I started by walking down the aisle as a bride at Saint Anthony's Church in Lowell, Massachusetts. Fast forward 10 years and I am walking down the aisle of an airplane with all my favorites and a paddleboard strapped to my back. Embarking into my next decade, the next chapter of my life!

In those 10 years, I got married; I flipped a copper penny, heads – get married, or tails – work a year on a cruise ship in the Hawaiian Islands. I was in love with the idea of stability and security and was hoping it would work out... It lasted 3.5 years! It just was not going to work. We were of different kinds! Ignoring that little intuitive feeling that there was something off, didn't really work out. **I have learned to be honest with myself.** Amidst that relationship, I was laid off and made a career change. I decided to take my experience in social work and my organizing hobby to the next level by **guiding others through their decluttering and organizing processes with their homes and businesses, all the while helping them heal through the process and realize that living with intention is greater than living with the things you hold on to.** Being honest with myself, love and light do not come from settling for what will work in this realm. **Our comfort zone is our personal prison, and it takes courage to move forward.** Moving on from relationships has created space for me to declutter and organize my world in a physical way in order to make space for my emotions and journey to continue. You see, the work you put into going through your belongings is 2-fold as it takes place both externally and internally.

Some experiences have been more traumatic than others, through which I have learned to forgive with no strings attached. Meaning that **I am responsible to answer for my actions ONLY and release energy that is not mine to carry or let others dictate my self-worth.**

A quarter of a century into life began my traumatizing experience in the world of the deaf, and by the age of 38, I had a Cochlear Implant. **God obviously wanted me to hear something I was not currently hearing.** This process led me to spend lots of time alone while surrounded by others without realizing it, and I was thereby blessed with self-awareness. I learned to read lips and read human energy without the words and noise, realizing that our intentions and feelings are the energy we carry. It is easier to decipher our connections to each other and see where and how God uses us as tools for goodness when we silence the noise. Residual hearing loss and the process of acknowledging where sound comes from, people's voices, recalibrating hearing, etc. set me in an imbalance that I had to recalibrate in order to become well again. The process evoked depression! I was waiting to be saved; yet everyday slipping deeper into the darkness, until February 27th 2019. It was on that very day that I was guided by a stronger force to surrender. It was a raw moment! I found myself in a helpless puddle of tears, mostly naked on a very cold New England winter morning, asking God to take the wheel as I automatically jumped into the co-pilot seat. **The awakening to realize that I am not in control yet to understand that I have to do what I have to do while still managing free will.** I felt called to open a daily devotional book (The Confident Woman Devotional by Joyce Meyer) that I had somehow acquired and read the message for that day, titled "God's Approval." **Submit yourselves, therefore, to God. Resist the devil, and he will flee from you. James 4:7.** Another opportunity to plummet into the inner job. Being depressed was from the beginning to the end of my journey into darkness. I lost sight of who I was and was quickly losing sight of the meaning of life. Then the calm arrived! This was the fertile soil of my growth thus far.

Once I surrendered to the Will of God and allowed the Universe, the angels, and all that is guiding me in the right direction to take control, all I had to do was put myself in neutral and "enjoy the ride." This ultimate feeling of freedom and liberation is made possible via the combination of working inwardly as well as outwardly simultaneously by way of identifying what is of service to me and to my purpose. I now truly understand that my purpose is to raise the vibration of the world so that humanity is set at a higher frequency – the frequency of love, joy, enlightenment, and BLISS.

During the last five years of the past 10 years, I slowed it down! Disconnecting from the world, one human and one thing at a time, it was time to self-examine, quiet the noise of the world, and learn to connect with the core of the earth, myself, and the Divine. In this light, I have implemented some daily practices such as: yoga, breath work, child play, prayer (talking to God) and meditation (listening to God). Learning the way back to myself, to the beautiful person and energy God created me to be. Through this process, I unprogrammed so much of what I had been programmed by society and the world. Only then was I able to plunge right into who I really am. That's where the hard work, "the inside job," comes into play. It is not an easy process to shed layers one at a time and deeper and deeper as you go. Many times, in the back of our closets are heavy old boxes of things that need to be accounted for and disposed of. I am talking about spring-cleaning, my friends! It was a complete assessment and inventory of what I had going on at the physical, psychological and spiritual levels.

In the physical realm, I became in tune with my body (learning it), finances, emails, voicemails, paperwork, chachkies, clothes, equipment, electronics, DVDs... ALL of it! Deciding what still serves a purpose and what is dead weight. Figuring out what is of value at this moment in time and will support my higher self and purpose. Detachment is not as easy as it seems, as we are emotionally attached to things, to people, and to the things that people gift us. **The major take away: Does it serve? Is it used in your daily life? Do you love it because it takes you to a moment of joy or supports your higher self's vision for you?** Parting ways and the lesson of detachment from the physical world, people, and the story of how the future was going to be and what life was going to look like - just let it be what it is – I am enough! Security does not come from circumstance and/or someone else. It comes from within and has been provided by God; it is "God confidence!" I have become aware that we are socially conditioned and comatose by society. Believing that if we conform, consume, and comply that we will be respected, accepted, and loved... our cup can and will never be filled by this physical world.

In the psychological realm, I became in tune with learning my truth, the one I was born with, the one that is innocent, the light of Christ! I didn't do this alone. No one needs to. Use your resources. Create a trustworthy inner circle that offers feedback with no judgment.

In the spiritual realm, I became in tune with my connection to God, the I AM! The connection to yourself as I AM! God is Love; therefore, I AM LOVE! See how God did that.... He created us in His image!

Is there a lack of knowledge of who you are because you have been bombarded with relationships, feelings, experiences, traditions, transitions, things, things, and so many THINGS? Are you so buried under all the stuff, emotionally, mentally, and physically? Letting go of the physical in order to honor our core. So often we feel the void and feverishly try to fill it with an event to plan, plans with friends, a tattoo, a cigarette, a new relationship, a drink, a vacation, a trip, a new outfit, a shopping spree, and the list goes on and on and on and then you need a Tania to come over to help get rid of the clutter that did not fill the void but yet suffocated you and wasted your resources: time, money, and energy, to name three of the big ones. Humanity is suffering with the effects of this "Great Imbalance." The world as we know it is experiencing a tipping point where the physical world has taken the reigns, sacrificed the mind and soul, and taken each one of us as its hostage. We live in a fog of understanding... that the world is suffering due to each and every one of us forgetting that we are spiritual beings, who were given the gift of a physical experience and not the other way around. Most are in a trance that we are all physical beings, and perhaps some special or chosen ones get to experience this extraordinary spiritual experience. In truth, the spiritual far surpasses the physical. One's connection to the Divine and to oneself is one in the same. That is why it has been so important to uncover and understand who I am and why I tick the way I do to the beat of my own drum.

The process to vibe at the highest is a unique journey for each individual, but the secret is to find one's balance, one's own beat. Some of the practices I have found myself doing are through nourishing my body with wholesome foods, listening to healing music, being in a space that is tidy and free from clutter, accepting my whole self and accepting others exactly for who they are while understanding that they are on their own journey. The balance is in one's caring for oneself, self-love but not as much as boasting, because then you've surpassed the threshold. This process does not happen overnight. It required me to take time to self-examine and accept who I am – all of me, the good and the bad – to forgive and let go – to decluttering and organizing the space around me and within me. Accept yourself and shed your light on the world. Your light is a gift from God to use for good and to be an example for others! Bad news... Satan will also be equipping you with his tools, such as pride, arrogance, jealousy, loneliness, failure, shame, low self-esteem, low self-value, and vanity to identify a few. But his biggest one is fear! What are you afraid of? Going out and conquering each and every one of our fears is where the healing begins. Clearing the trauma, one at a time! I like to imagine myself holding a bundle of red balloons as I wear a beautiful flowy white dress and some awesome red heels. I begin to cut each cord with compassion, acceptance, love, intention, and gratitude to let go of any hold it ever had on me. "Bless and release!" By going into a meditative state, grounding myself, connecting with my higher self in gratitude to God, I am giving Him all of the glory. I have a garden in my being. It's a place where I often retreat to. A place that is good and has a high vibration. It has beautiful clear skies, a sun that beams brightly, and warmth that heals the soul. A magical place filled with wildflowers of all colors at the edge of a body of water where a bench invites me to sit next to my higher self in Jesus' form. A quick physical touch, a sign of peace and sacred energy of the highest vibration is exchanged. Quieting the world's fog/noise has been imperative to my self-discovery and growth.

Acceptance of oneself and bringing your bag of "junk" to the foot of the cross, having compassion on yourself and others, "Namaste – I honor the place in you in which the entire universe dwells. I honor the place in you, that is of love, light, peace, and joy. When you are in that place in you and I am in that place in me – WE ARE ONE." How do you get to "that place" in you? Jesus said to him, "I am the way, and the truth, and the life. No one comes to the Father except through me." John 14:6 "For there is one God, and there is one mediator between God and men, the man Christ Jesus." Timothy 2:5 The closer you get to your core the closer you get to God. God doesn't make junk. When God made mankind, He said it was "Very Good!" In fact, the Bible describes God's views of you this way:

- You are the Apple of His eye – Can't get much better than that ~ Psalm 17:18
- You were worth Dying for – He paid the ultimate price for you ~ John 15:13
- He gave His Best for you – His only begotten Son ~ Romans 8:32
- He thinks of you All the time – Even when you're asleep ~ Psalms 40:5
- He takes it personally when anyone offends you – That's deep! ~ Matthew 25:40
- He's assigned **YOU** Personal Body Guards – Yep... Angels ~ Psalm 34:7

How do you find balance? It's ironic that many times it takes losing your balance to find it. On your mark, get set, recalibrate. When life starts to tip due to death, divorce, layoff, etc. Whatever the circumstance, that is all it is, but balance must be found. Today, I have recalibrated. Are you ready for an alignment – body, mind, and soul? I find myself in a state of bliss of being free from stuff, moving freely through circumstances and the world, understanding that if I can manage to quiet the noise just enough to follow my intuition and have the courage to follow the calling, God will always provide!

Letting life live through me as it is my duty to follow my intuition and enjoy the journey, all the feels; the lows and the highs. For it is in the valley that the soil is fertile, and there are so many lessons and tools that are provided to us that if we do not take the time and consciousness to recognize them and appreciate the lesson. We will have to pay interest on understanding the circumstance and how it fits into our so-called puzzle of life. God uses me as a tool, as a bridge. He uses me as an example of unconditional love and compassion wherever I go, but only if I follow Him. What does this mean? Follow the light, lean into what is good, and love on others and on the world regardless of how it has or is treating you. God will always lead you; the answers are embedded within your soul. Soul searching occurs when one takes time to speak (pray) and listen (meditate). Soon after that, you begin to feel and connect with your intuition (that inner voice, that feeling, that pull, that leap of faith), what some call the mystery of faith. Follow that call/intuition and God promises to supply you with all that you need.

Creators of our own Universe and the magic of manifestation. I have gained an understanding of the body, mind, soul, and being in connection with the Divine is the core to wellbeing. It is as I have unlocked a secret passage in my life through my daily practices; study (workshops, classes, seminars, sharing prospective with others), prayer (speaking to God)/meditation (Listening to God), yoga (creating space internally), daily devotional & breath work (The Art of Living) – The journey to grounding and centering my body, mind and soul.

Your support! Your tribe! Your community! It is imperative to be surrounded by those who are examples of what unconditional love looks like in this realm, for they are our earthly angels. They support us and love us despite our brokenness. They are also fertile soil for us to grow into who God has created us to be. I have been vigilant and caught the signs - the repeating numbers, the symbols I come across, the shapes in the clouds, all of them. The angels continue to guide and protect me, and as I see the signs, not only do I recognize them, I take the time to thank them for providing me with unconditional confirmation that I am on the right path and that the love that is poured out of me is not ever in vain.

My journey has brought me back home and the knowledge of whose approval I need, and that is not of Man. I am centered, grounded, and at peace! I have been living by intuition, that call. I have leaped into the mystery of faith! I once was asked, "Are you open to being open?" My answer is "YES!" Interestingly enough, I am currently on the itty-bitty little island of Graciosa (Graceland), located in the midst of the Atlantic Ocean between the United States and mainland Portugal. Embracing all experiences God places in my path! One of which will be experiencing some volunteer work in Lisbon, Portugal through International Volunteer HQ. Having the courage to do what fills my cup is purely through the Grace of God. I am completely at God's Will! It is bliss to follow His path, my way!

I recognize that I am a member of Christ's body, which has given me the strength and grace to face the situation at hand with love and compassion as I travel through this journey on a path that is unique to me! So, if you can be anything, be kind to those whose journeys are being affected by your encounter. Send them off to raise their vibration. We are not only responsible for taking on this difficult task of "the inside job," but also to set an example to our future generations on how to do it with love, compassion, and grace! I am only responsible for my inside job. You cannot change anyone but yourself, but you can change and show up for yourself as you lead others by being an example. It's not an easy process. The odds are against you, but by the same token, you are highly favored by God.

My gift to humanity is to help guide and support others through their own journey back home! There is an amazing movement that is happening – God is strengthening His people and calling us home, by name, one-by-one. "Ask and it shall be given." Pray with all of your might, ask for guidance! "For God so loved the world, that he gave his only begotten Son, that whoever believeth in him should not perish, but have everlasting life." John 3:16 He did this so that we would all have an example of how to love and be in the frequency of love. How to walk amongst sinners and be able to lead. Let us elevate the vibration of the world placing it into the frequency of love, peace, enlightenment and BLISS – the rewards of completing the inside job!

The Lord your God is with you,
He is mighty to save.
He will take great delight in you,
He will quiet you with his love,
He will rejoice over you with singing.
Zephaniah 3:17

About the Author
TANIA ORMONDE

Tania Ormonde, the optimizer, brings magic into your world! She is passionate and committed to transforming the way one lives and feels within their space.

Tania thrives in helping individuals optimize their lifestyle while creating an environment where they find their brightest light in a clutter-free space. Providing calmness and peace to one's mind and soul, while allowing mental and spiritual vibrations to rise. In turn welcoming and hosting higher frequency energy in a space of acceptance, love, and joy where you vibe at your highest.

She holds over a decade of experience in decluttering and optimizing in the way we live and feel. Her once personal hobby has since become her way of life!

She has been exposed to life and culture in several countries and experienced the world as her playground. Tania holds a degree in Cultural Geography, 10 years in social work, and a lifetime of personal development. She has been a guest speaker for Maddie Sparkles on "Intuition, a conscious conversation" as well as "Decluttering and Organizing Your Life and Business" for Windham Women's Business Connection. Tania continues to be active as a monthly speaker and coach for "The Art of Organizing Workshop" at Brigid's Crossing, a young mother's nonprofit organization.

In everything Tania does, she does it with love! Liberate yourself and simplify your life!

Connect with Tania
Facebook link:
www.facebook.com/Declutter-Optimize-101127095902438

Instagram link:
www.instagram.com/declutter_and_optimize/

Linkedin:
www.linkedin.com/in/taniaormonde

Inspired Hearts
Publishing

Inspired Hearts Publishing is passionate about sharing inspiring stories of men and women who've overcome great hardships, experienced untraditional success, and are carving out their own path in life—stories of hope, inspiration, strength, resilience, love, and transformation.

We thrive on providing a platform for business owners to leverage their personal story, experience, and expertise to grow their audience and establish themselves as an expert in their industry.

If you loved this book, please give us a 5 star review on Amazon or GoodReads
and
Send us an email at write@inspiredheartspublishing.com.

SCAN ME

Manufactured by Amazon.ca
Bolton, ON